Hannah Miles

traybakes

40 brilliant one-tin bakes for enjoying, selling and giving

LORENZ BOOKS

Let the recipes in this book inspire you
to create some tempting treats that everyone will love.

CONTENTS

INTRODUCTION

Traybakes are one of the simplest forms of cakes and are always a firm favourite. The joy of a traybake is that it can be prepared in very little time and then can be cut into slices and squares to serve or sell – and of course to eat! The traybakes all transport easily in their tin and are just right for offering up at a bake sale.

Everyone loves to eat cake and bake stalls are therefore a very good way of raising money for good causes, be it a school fête, a street party or a church sale. This book contains a wide variety of treats perfect for selling and baking in bulk, and of course just for enjoying. Each recipe makes 24 cakes, but don't worry if you want to bake on a larger or smaller scale, the ingredients are easy to adjust up or down.

The important thing to remember for bake sales and fêtes is to keep everything simple – there is no need to make really highly decorated cakes as generally these are cakes to be enjoyed on the spot. This does not mean that you can't have fun with decoration, but bear in mind that not only do you need to take your goods to the event, but that some people may want to take them home as well so they should be transportable.

It is also important to think about offering some lower-calorie treats – there is no need to scrimp on flavour and taste however and the Virtuous chapter at the end of this book contains a delectable variety of healthy treats which also cater for common allergies with dairy-free and gluten-free traybakes.

If you love to bake, then why not plan a fundraising sale and make the most of your talents. Have fun whilst baking, knowing it is all for a good cause. Let the recipes in this book inspire you to create some tempting treats that everyone will love.

Make your traybakes look attractive so they sell well.

Line the trays and plates the cakes are displayed on with paper napkins or doilies.

TOP TIPS FOR A BAKE SALE

1 You need to be able to easily transport your traybakes from home to the sale. You can either transport them in the tin that you bake them in and then cut into pieces at the sale, or alternatively cut into pieces at home and transport in cake cases on a tray all ready to display. Make sure that decorations are not so fragile that they will be damaged in transit.

2 Your traybakes need to look attractive so that they sell well. Pretty sweets, candies, icing and sugar flowers all make cakes look very appealing. In addition, you can line the trays and plates the cakes are displayed on with paper napkins or doilies.

3 Keep your traybakes simple. Although the traybake needs to be attractive, there is no need for really fancy cakes with delicate decorations as these are likely to suffer when they are cut into. People love all the easy classics – Victoria sponge, red velvet, classic chocolate – and these are the cakes that tend to sell best.

4 Bakes need to be easy to cut into individual portions. Avoid cakes that are hard to serve or are messy to eat as people need to be able to easily buy and eat individual cake portions.

5 Choose appropriate recipes. If you are baking for a school cake sale you may want to avoid a traybake that contains nuts. Some schools are introducing regulations about sugar levels on foods and so it would be appropriate to choose a low-sugar recipe and to label the traybake clearly. Check what you are making is suitable for the sale or recipient.

6 Have clear labelling. It is helpful to list out ingredients so people with dietary requirements can see what's included, or to fit local regulations. People want to know what's in a cake and what it costs without having to ask.

7 Keep pricing simple. An easy rounded figure makes the maths much easier, and don't forget price signs for the cakes. Sometimes it is easier to have all the cakes at the same price to help with the maths.

8 Make sure you have plenty of change. Fête organizers sometimes provide a float but if not your bank will be able to provide coins for your float in exchange for notes.

9 Price the cakes to sell. Although you want to make a profit, do not overprice your cakes as you do not want to be left with any at the end of the day, they won't keep until the next sale. If it is getting late in the day and you still have lots left, reduce your prices or offer 2 for the price of 1.

10 Try to plan for variety. If people are volunteering donations of cakes see if you can try and steer them all in different directions so that you have a wide selection of cakes on sale.

11 Name your tray. Make sure you – or other bakers – label cake plates, stands and trays with a sticker underneath so you know who to return them to at the end of the sale and to avoid things getting lost.

12 Have fun and enjoy raising money for a good cause!

Use decorative labels to let people know what the cakes are and the prices.

Allow plenty of time to display things in the most appealing way.

CREATING A BEAUTIFUL DISPLAY

In order to ensure that your cakes sell well and raise as much money as possible at your bake sale, it is best to display things as prettily as possible for maximum "kerb appeal."

First begin by creating a pretty stall – use tablecloths to cover the tables and if available hang bunting along the edge of the table and above your stand. Make a creative sign letting everyone know that you are selling cakes – stencilling and decoupage work well and if you love to sew you could even appliqué a "Cake Sale" sign. Although it takes time to make you can use it again and again.

Have decorative but clear labels – let people know what the cakes are and the prices. If you want you can make a "cake menu" to hand out to people, describing the choice of cakes available. Chalk boards also work well for displaying what you have to offer and prices, the beauty being that you can simply rub out when cakes sell out.

If possible label allergens and identify which cakes are suitable for allergy sufferers – such as dairy-free and gluten-free cakes. It is important to check that you comply with any food labelling rules in the country in which you are selling.

Incorporate shelves or tiered stands – adding height and different levels on your stand creates variety in the display and will make your stall look more attractive. You can present bags of biscuits and cookies in pretty wicker baskets or in boxes lined with tissue paper.

Think about the variety of cakes – if your cakes are made up of donations and you are reliant on the good will of people to kindly donate cakes, then you are unlikely to be able to have much input on the variety of cakes on offer. However if you are making the cakes with a group of organized volunteers why not have a meeting together and plan what you are all going to make to ensure that you have a good mix of both flavours and varieties of cakes and cookies. Do you want to sell whole cakes as well as individual portions?

Practical considerations – make sure that everyone who is baking for your stall knows what time they have to deliver by. I usually tell people a time slightly earlier than my actual cut off time to allow for people running late and also to allow plenty of time to display things in the most appealing way.

Have spare plates, cake cases, sharp knives and a spatula available in case people deliver cakes without cutting them. I also like to have a piping bag on hand and some sugar sprinkles in case of emergencies – you never know when they will come in handy for any cakes damaged in transit!

PRICING, LABELLING AND TRANSPORTING PRODUCTS FOR SALE

PRICING YOUR TRAYBAKES

For someone who loves to bake, pricing and working out the costs to charge for cakes is one of my least favourite things! For me, it is all about the sharing and enjoying. That said, whilst it may be dull, where you are seeking to raise funds or to make a profit it is most definitely worth taking time to calculate the right costs to charge.

When pricing you need to balance two things. Firstly to make sure that all your costs are covered and that you make a profit on top; and secondly to make sure that your goods are affordable.

If people have donated cakes to your stall then you do not need to carry out calculations to ensure that your costs are covered. Simply judge what people are likely to pay for the cakes by thinking about what you would be prepared to pay for them yourself. Perhaps 20 pence/50 cents for small cakes and £1/$1.50 for a slice of a large cake or a beautifully decorated cupcake. Whole large cakes will generally sell for around £3–5/$4.50–7.50.

If you are paying for the ingredients for your bakes out of the profit, you need to calculate the cost of the ingredients to make sure that you cover your costs. To do this, calculate the rough cost of the quantity of ingredient that your recipe calls for. For example if a recipe calls for 500g/1¼lb of flour and a 1.5kg/3½lb bag of flour costs £1.20, the price you need to include for your costing is 40 pence. Do the same with all the other ingredients and then divide the total quantity by 24 so that you get a price per cake. Then add to this the profit you want to make on each cake. Generally making 50–100% profit would be what you are aiming for.

You don't want to overprice your items so that they do not sell and you have lots of cakes left over at the end of the sale. Have a variety of pricing levels so that you have something for every pocket. Children will often bring their pocket money and will want to buy something themselves, so make sure that you have some cheaper cakes and cookies available as well.

Try
me I'M
delicious!

LABELLING YOUR TRAYBAKES

A label can be informative as well as attractive, as people can need to know what's in the bake. A descriptive title tempts them to buy, and a list of the main ingredients can be useful.

It is a good idea to have a few allergy-friendly traybakes to offer, however you do need to be careful that they are labelled correctly. With items such as dairy-free or egg-free cakes this is relatively easy as it is simply a question of omitting those items from the recipe, but with gluten-free recipes this can be more difficult as there can be trace element particles of flour in the air and on kitchen equipment unless you cook in a completely gluten-free environment.

For this reason you need to be extremely careful about labelling. If you do not bake in a gluten-free environment there are now strict regulations on allergen labelling in some countries, with limits on the low level of gluten that can be contained in products before they can be labelled "Gluten-free". If you can't meet these standards then it may be better to label the products as "no gluten-containing ingredients". Given that this is a specialized area, I recommend that you take advice from the Food Standards Agency or equivalent in your country who will be able to assist you in how to correctly label your products for sale.

I love to use ground almonds in baking, particularly in gluten-free cakes as they give a good texture. However some people are allergic to nuts and occasionally school fêtes can ban nuts altogether for safety. If this is the case you can substitute the quantity of ground almonds with regular flour or ground sunflower seeds which work well. You can omit the nut decoration on the cakes as they will still taste good.

If you want, you could note the calorie count per slice. The nutritional information is all detailed at the back of the book. You might decide to do this for the lower-calorie 'virtuous' traybakes in the last chapter!

TRANSPORTING YOUR TRAYBAKES

No matter how carefully you drive or walk, moving cakes and keeping their decorations intact can be difficult. I transport cupcakes on high-sided trays and lightly cover the top with foil. If you cover tightly with clear film or plastic wrap the icing will likely get squashed and your decorative efforts will be ruined.

If you have made a traybake you can transport this easily in the tin or pan you baked it in and then cut into slices when you arrive at your destination.

Good kitchen and baking stores now sell a variety of cupcake and cake carriers, with plastic lids and handles for carrying, which are ideal, so if you bake regularly you may wish to invest in these.

BAKING FOR SPECIAL DIETS

Nowadays so many people have allergies – I am not sure whether it is because we are becoming more intolerant to ingredients or because there is a higher level of diagnosis, but whichever it is, it is important at a bake sale to cater for allergies if you can and provide some alternative cakes and treats.

If I am holding a bake sale I usually try to make at least one dairy-free cake and one gluten-free cake. You will make someone's day if they find they can actually have a slice of cake from your stall. The Virtuous chapter in this book contains a good selection of dairy-free and egg-free cakes as well as gluten-free cakes, and there are also several gluten-free cakes in the other chapters, such as flapjacks and brownies (although do note that some people who are allergic to gluten cannot eat oats and so you need to ensure that you use gluten-free oats).

If you are baking for people with allergies it is so important to read the packaging on your ingredients to ensure that they do not contain trace elements. For gluten-free baking, areas to be particularly careful about are dried fruits and glacé/candied cherries, as these can sometimes contain a wheat-based anti-caking agent to prevent the fruit from sticking. Baking powder is sometimes bulked with wheat flour (although many manufacturers are now using rice flour) and also icing/confectioners' sugar which can contain a wheat-based anti-caking agent. Also be careful with chocolates as some contain milk powders which again can contain wheat.

For those with dairy allergies, some are allergic to lactose contained in dairy products and if this is the case there is a wide variety of lactose-free products, such as yogurts and baking spreads, which are suitable to use. For those who are truly allergic to all dairy, cakes can be made with oil instead.

LOW-CALORIE BAKING

If I am honest, cakes are never going to be really healthy and as an occasional treat there is no harm in indulging in something delicious and calorie-laden. That said, for those who are watching their weight it is possible to easily adapt most of the recipes in this book and make skinnier versions following the hints and tips below.

- The skinny blueberry and cinnamon cake on page 110 has only 68 calories per slice and you can easily adapt the flavours in the base cake for other very skinny treats.

- One simple way to lower the calories is to make smaller servings of the cake – so rather than cutting each slice into 24, cut into 30 instead, which will make each cake lower in calories (which is fine as long as you don't then eat 2!). Sometimes just a small mouthful is enough for a treat.

- In place of butter, substitute dairy-free or very low-fat baking spread instead. It is important to check that the spread you select is suitable for baking as some of them are not – it will usually say this clearly on the side of the packet. Using a spread which is not suitable for baking will potentially mean that your cake will not bake properly so take care you use the correct product.

- In place of full-fat/full cream milk, use skimmed or zero-fat milk and in place of yogurt or sour cream, use zero-fat or low-fat natural yogurt for equally delicious results.

- In place of full-fat cream cheese use low-fat cream cheese instead.

- You can also try reducing the sugar quantity slightly in recipes to reduce the calorie content and make a less sweet version.

STORING TRAYBAKES

It has to be said that cakes are always best on the day they are made, although a lot of recipes in this book will keep well for a few days if stored correctly. Each recipe gives storage instructions.

Cakes will normally keep well for 2 days but are even better fresh, so I normally do not bake them any sooner than the day before my sale, or preferably on the morning of the sale depending on how much time you have.

- Store cakes in airtight containers or leave them in the tin they were baked in and once cool, wrap tightly in clear film/plastic wrap.

- Brownies and blondies, flapjack and traybake slices will all keep well and will store for at least 3 days in an airtight container.

- If you bake on a large scale regularly, it is worth investing in some decent storage tins – either metal or tight-sealing plastic boxes.

- If the slice contains fresh cream, cream cheese or other fresh dairy products or fresh fruit, they can be stored in the refrigerator wrapped in clear film. Cakes containing fresh cream really should be eaten on the day they are made.

LINING TINS AND PANS

As all of the slices and little cakes will need to be removed from their tins before serving, it is important to line the cake tins and pans you use carefully to make sure that your treats can be lifted out easily and don't get stuck.

The recipes in this book are all made in a 35 x 25cm/14 x 10in deep rectangular baking tin which is a good size and shape for making and cutting 24 portions of each cake or slice. But you can vary the tin if required, and the following instructions explain how to line different-shaped tins.

To line square or rectangular tins cut a sheet of baking parchment slightly larger than the size of your tin. Grease the tin with butter. Place your tin in the centre of your paper and using small

scissors cut diagonally from each paper corner to the corner of the tin. Place the paper in the greased tin and overlap the cut corners so that the paper fits neatly into the tin.

To line deep round or square tins cut a long strip of baking parchment slightly deeper than the tin and long enough to go round the whole tin. Fold a 2.5cm/1in fold along the length of the paper and snip small incisions along the strip. Cut a circle or square of baking parchment the size of the bottom of the tin. Grease the tin with butter and then insert the strip of baking parchment around the inside of the tin so that the snipped fringe lies flat on the bottom of the tin. Place the parchment circle or square into the tin to cover the fringe.

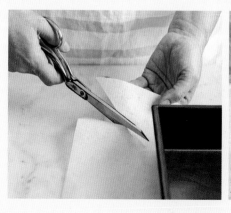

SOME
BASIC INGREDIENTS

The majority of recipes in this book use core larder ingredients that I always have in my store cupboard. As a general rule I like to have the following readily available: plain/all-purpose flour and self-raising/self-rising flour; fresh eggs; butter, margarine or low-fat baking spread; natural/plain yogurt and cream cheese; caster/superfine sugar and dark brown sugar; good-quality chocolate and some chocolate chips; golden/light corn syrup; oats; and a selection of nuts and dried fruits. With these simple ingredients you will be able to whip up a delicious traybake in virtually no time at all.

SOME BASIC BAKING TECHNIQUES

Baking is a simple process and as long as you follow the key steps you will be able to rustle up delicious cakes and treats at the drop of a hat. The guidelines below show you how to make an essential sponge cake, frostings, ganache and a biscuit base.

MAKING A SPONGE CAKE

1 Mix together the butter and sugar until very light and creamy using a stand mixer or whisk. It is important to continue whisking until the mixture goes from golden yellow to very pale as this adds lots of air to your mixture and will ensure the cake rises well.

2 Add the eggs one at a time and whisk after each is added. If the mixture starts to curdle, do not worry, simply add a tablespoon of flour to the batter from the quantity you will add later from the recipe. Continue until all the eggs are added.

3 Sift in the flour and fold in gently either with the mixer on its lowest speed setting or using a spatula.

4 Add in a drizzle of yogurt, milk or sour cream which will add moisture to the cake.

5 Stir the mixture thoroughly with a spatula. Spoon the mixture into your tin/pan.

6 Bake at the temperature in the recipe until the cake springs back to your touch if you press in the centre with a clean finger and a knife inserted into the centre comes out clean with no cake batter on.

7 Leave the cake to cool in the tin for a few minutes as it can be fragile when it first comes out of the oven, and then turn out on to a rack to cool.

Sponge cake technique

Buttercream or cream cheese frosting

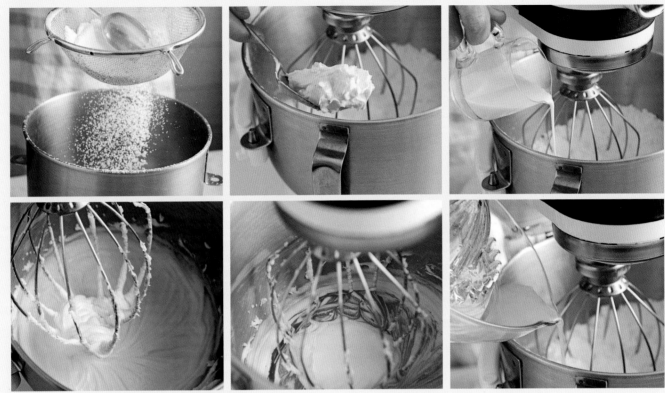

MAKING BUTTERCREAM OR CREAM CHEESE FROSTING

1 It is important to make sure that your butter or cream cheese are at room temperature and easily spreadable. If it is hard you will end up with small lumps in your buttercream which is not pleasant at all!

2 Sift the icing/confectioners' sugar into a bowl. Add the butter or cream cheese to the bowl. Using an electric mixer, whisk or beater, start to whisk very slowly at first (take care that the icing/confectioners' sugar does not explode in a dust cloud).

3 If called for in the recipe, add the milk gradually until the icing is thick and stiff and holds a peak when you lift up the beater.

4 Then whisk for a good few minutes until it becomes light and airy. If it is too stiff and hard to beat add a little more milk and whisk again. If you add too much milk and it does not hold a peak, simply add a little more icing sugar and whisk in again until you have the right consistency.

5 You can flavour your buttercream – for instance with vanilla, cocoa powder, peppermint extract or citrus juice – and you can colour it with your chosen food colouring (see hint and tip below) – the possibilities are endless.

Hint and tip

There are many different types of food colouring available – liquids, pastes and gels. Some are made with natural colouring and you may prefer to use these. The colour obtained may not be as strong using these or liquid food colouring. I use gel colours and AmeriColor gel pastes are available in good cake shops and online – I find these give the most vibrant colour.

Chocolate ganache

MAKING CHOCOLATE GANACHE

1 To melt chocolate, break the chocolate into pieces and place in a heatproof bowl. Add the correct quantity of cream and butter called for in the recipe. Place the bowl over a pan of simmering water. Take care that the bottom of the bowl does not touch the water and also that the water does not get into the chocolate as it can cause the chocolate to split and go grainy.

2 Heat until the chocolate and butter have melted, stirring occasionally.

3 Remove from the heat and stir to form a thick glossy ganache. Spread the ganache over the top of your cake.

Biscuit base

MAKING A BISCUIT BASE

1 Place the biscuits or cookies in a clean plastic bag with no holes – a sealable sandwich bag is ideal. Bash with a rolling pin until you have fine crumbs – this is very good therapy I find! Alternatively you can do this in a food processor or blender.

2 Melt the butter in a pan over the heat, cool slightly and then stir into the biscuit crumbs so that they are all coated.

3 Press the crumbs into the base of the tin with the back of a spoon in an even layer. Leave to chill in the refrigerator until it is needed.

TRAYBAKE
Cakes

These are the true traybakes, delicious squares of cake in all the classic flavours. Most cakes in this chapter can be prepared in less than 40 minutes and make great centrepiece slices for your fête table.

All the popular family recipes are here – from red velvet cake to a banana sheet cake – as well as treats from around the world such as lamingtons, pumpkin gingerbread and fruity crumble. Seasonal themes are catered for too, with a wave-the-flag traybake and spooky chocolate-orange squares for Halloween.

Cakes are everyone's favourite and the recipes in this chapter are sure to delight.

I don't know anyone who doesn't love a good red velvet cake.

The tang of passion fruit curd balances the sweet blackberries perfectly.

Gingerbread used to be my Grandad Goodwin's favourite cake and whenever I bake it I remember him fondly.

RED VELVET
with cream cheese frosting

I don't know anyone who doesn't love a good red velvet cake – it has such a vibrant shade, created by the dark cocoa and red food colouring. This cake is always topped with a classic cream cheese frosting which is a perfect foil for the deep rich cake.

PREPARATION TIME 25 minutes
BAKING TIME 25–30 minutes
MAKES 24

EQUIPMENT 35 x 25cm/14 x 10in deep baking tin/pan, greased and lined, piping/pastry bag fitted with a star nozzle
PREHEAT THE OVEN TO 180°C/350°F/Gas 4

FOR THE CAKE

340g/12oz/1½ cups caster/superfine sugar

340g/12oz/2 sticks 6 tbsp butter, margarine or low-fat baking spread, softened

6 eggs

340g/12oz/2½ cups self-raising/self-rising flour, sifted

60g/2oz/½ cup cocoa powder, sifted

150ml/¼ pint/⅔ cup sour cream

1 tsp/5ml red food colouring gel

FOR THE FROSTING

600g/1lb 5oz/5½ cups icing/confectioners' sugar, sifted

100g/3½oz low-fat cream cheese

60g/2oz/4 tbsp butter, softened

Juice of 1 lemon

Cocoa powder, to dust

Red sugar sprinkles

1. To prepare the sponge, whisk together the caster sugar and the butter in a mixing bowl using a mixer or whisk until light and creamy. Add the eggs and whisk again. Fold in the sifted flour and cocoa. Add the sour cream and food colouring and whisk gently so that the cake has an even deep red-brown colour.

2. Spoon the mixture into the prepared cake tin and smooth out level using a spatula.

3. Bake in the preheated oven for 25–30 minutes until the cake is firm and springs back to your touch. Remove from the oven and leave to cool for a few minutes, then turn out on to a rack to cool completely.

4. For the frosting, place the sifted icing sugar, cream cheese, butter and lemon juice into a mixing bowl and whisk together until thick and creamy. If the frosting is too stiff add a little more lemon juice and if it is too runny add a little more icing sugar. The consistency of the icing will depend on how soft your butter and cream cheese are.

5. Cut the cake into 24 pieces. Spoon the frosting into the piping bag and pipe a swirl of icing on to each piece of cake. Dust with a little cocoa powder and decorate with the sugar sprinkles and transfer to the refrigerator for an hour or so for the icing to set. This cake will keep for up to 2 days in an airtight container.

BANANA
sheet cake

Everyone likes banana cake – this one is rich and dense and has a lovely oaty topping and juicy sultanas. It is important that the bananas you use are very ripe – it is best to wait until their skins begin to turn black.

PREPARATION TIME 10 minutes
BAKING TIME 35–40 minutes
MAKES 24

3 ripe bananas

340g/12oz/1½ cups caster/superfine sugar

340g/12oz/2 sticks 6 tbsp butter, margarine or low-fat baking spread, softened

6 eggs

2 tsp/10ml ground cinnamon

175ml/6fl oz/¾ cup low-fat Greek/US strained plain yogurt

400g/14oz/scant 3 cups self-raising/self-rising flour, sifted

170g/6oz sultanas/golden raisins

30g/1oz/⅓ cup porridge/rolled oats

1 tbsp/15ml caster/superfine sugar

1 tsp/5ml mixed/apple pie spice

EQUIPMENT 35 x 25cm/14 x 10in deep baking tin/pan, greased and lined
PREHEAT THE OVEN TO 180°C/350°F/Gas 4

1 Crush the bananas with a fork until they are soft. To prepare the sponge, whisk together the caster sugar, butter and banana in a mixing bowl using a mixer or whisk until light and creamy. Add the eggs and whisk again.

2 Fold in the ground cinnamon, yogurt and sifted flour. Fold in the sultanas and pour the batter into the lined tin and level with a spatula.

3 Mix together the oats, caster sugar and mixed spice and sprinkle over the top of the cake.

4 Bake in the preheated oven for 35–40 minutes until the cake is firm and springs back to your touch. Remove from the oven and leave to cool for a few minutes, then turn out on to a rack to cool completely.

5 When you are ready to serve, cut the cake into 24 slices. This cake will keep for up to 3 days in an airtight container.

Hint and tip
if your bananas are very ripe but you are not ready to bake, peel the banana and cut into slices and place in a sandwich bag in the freezer. Defrost before using.

GLAZED CINNAMON
apple slice

The combination of cinnamon and apple is an American classic, used in the most delicious apple pies. This recipe takes all these lovely apple pie flavours and turns them into a moist traybake cake that will always be popular at fêtes and fairs.

PREPARATION TIME 15 minutes
BAKING TIME 40–50 minutes
MAKES 24

340g/12oz/1¾ cups dark brown sugar

340g/12oz/2 sticks 6 tbsp butter, margarine or low-fat baking spread, softened

6 eggs

250g/9oz ricotta cheese

280g/10oz/2 cups self-raising/self-rising flour, sifted

200g/7oz/2 cups ground almonds

2 tsp/10ml ground cinnamon

1 tsp/5ml mixed/apple pie spice

115g/4oz raisins

600g/1lb 5oz baking apples (approx. 4–5)

Juice of 1 lemon

1 tbsp/15ml caster/superfine sugar to sprinkle over the apple

FOR THE GLAZE

100g/3½oz apricot glaze or apricot jam

Juice of 1 lemon

EQUIPMENT 35 x 25cm/14 x 10in deep baking tin/pan, greased and lined
PREHEAT THE OVEN TO 180°C/350°F/Gas 4

1 To prepare the sponge, whisk together the dark brown sugar and the butter in a mixing bowl using a mixer or whisk until light and creamy. Add the eggs and whisk again. Whisk in the ricotta. Fold in the sifted flour and ground almonds. Add the ground cinnamon and mixed spice and the raisins and stir in gently. Grate two of the apples. It is fine to leave the skins on but do not grate the core. Stir the grated apple into the cake mixture.

2 Spoon the mixture into the prepared cake tin and smooth out level using a spatula.

3 To prepare the topping, peel and core the remaining apples and cut into thin slices. Place the slices in a bowl and toss with the lemon juice to prevent the apple from browning. It is important to cut the apple thinly so that you have enough slices to cover the top of the cake. Arrange the apple slices over the top of the cake in decorative patterns. Sprinkle with the caster sugar.

4 Bake in the preheated oven for 40–50 minutes until the cake is firm and springs back to your touch. Remove from the oven.

5 For the glaze, place the apricot glaze or jam in a pan with the lemon juice and simmer over a gentle heat until the mixture is runny and the glaze/jam has dissolved. If using jam which contains pieces of fruit, pass the mixture through a sieve or strainer to remove them. Brush the glaze over the top of the apples using a pastry brush. Leave the cake to cool.

6 To serve, cut the cake into 24 slices. This cake will keep for up to 3 days in an airtight container but is best eaten on the day it is made.

Hint and tip

For a lower fat version 1) use low-fat baking spread in place of the butter 2) omit the ricotta cheese and replace with 300ml/½ pint/1¼ cups of low-fat yogurt, adding at the same time as the grated apple 3) omit the glaze if you want to reduce the calories.

PUMPKIN gingerbread

Gingerbread used to be my Grandad Goodwin's favourite cake and whenever I bake it I remember him fondly. This is a dense gingerbread, made lovely and moist by the addition of the pumpkin purée.

PREPARATION TIME 10 minutes
BAKING TIME 25–35 minutes
MAKES 24

EQUIPMENT 35 x 25cm/14 x 10in deep baking tin/pan, greased and lined
PREHEAT THE OVEN TO 180°C/350°F/Gas 4

550g/1lb 3oz/3⅔ cups plain/all-purpose flour

1 tsp/5ml baking powder

1 tsp/5ml bicarbonate of soda/baking soda

1 tsp/5ml ground cinnamon

1 tsp/5ml ground ginger

1 tsp/5ml ground mixed/pumpkin pie spice

1 tsp/5ml vanilla powder or vanilla extract

A pinch of salt

250g/9oz/2 sticks butter, margarine or low-fat baking spread

170g/6oz treacle/molasses

170g/6oz golden/light corn syrup

2 tbsp/30ml ginger syrup

150g/5oz/¾ cups soft dark brown sugar

175ml/6fl oz/¾ cup milk

400g/14oz pumpkin purée

250g/9oz Greek/US strained plain yogurt

2 eggs, beaten

Icing/confectioners' sugar, for dusting

Small white sugar pearls

1 Sift the flour into a large mixing bowl with the baking powder, bicarbonate of soda, spices, vanilla and salt.

2 In a pan heat the butter, treacle, syrups and dark brown sugar until the sugar has melted.

3 Remove from the heat and leave to cool slightly. Stir in the milk. Pour the syrup mixture into the flour mixture and whisk in. Whisk in the pumpkin purée, yogurt and eggs and then pour into the prepared tin.

4 Bake in the preheated oven for 25–35 minutes until the cake is firm and a knife comes out clean with no batter on when inserted into the centre of the cake.

5 To decorate, cut the cake into 24 squares and dust with icing sugar. For the cute gingerbread decoration, cut out a small man shape from a piece of paper as a template and place on a square of cake. Dust over icing sugar, then carefully remove the paper template. Press small white sugar pearls into the cakes as eyes and buttons. Repeat with the other squares. This cake will store in an airtight container for up to 3 days.

Hint and tip

If you cannot buy pumpkin purée or want to make your own, simply chop and peel a small pumpkin and discard the seeds (or clean and roast them to use in other baking recipes or as a snack). Preheat the oven to 190°C/375°F/Gas 5. Place the pumpkin on a large piece of double-layered foil with 45ml/3 tbsp maple syrup, wrap the foil up well and bake for 30–40 minutes until the pumpkin flesh is soft. Cool, then purée in a food processor. For a lower fat version of this recipe, use low-fat yogurt in place of the Greek yogurt and use skimmed milk.

ORANGE AND CHOCOLATE
layer cake

This chocolate and orange layer cake with a rich chocolate drizzle topping is the perfect cake to serve for Halloween parties. You can decorate it with sugar spiders and Halloween sprinkles for a spooky treat.

PREPARATION TIME 20 minutes
BAKING TIME 20–25 minutes
MAKES 24

340g/12oz/2 sticks 6 tbsp butter, margarine or low-fat baking spread, softened

340g/12oz/1½ cups caster/superfine sugar

6 eggs

340g/12oz/2½ cups self-raising/self-rising flour, sifted

150ml/¼ pint/⅔ cup buttermilk

Zest and juice of 2 small oranges

A few drops of orange food colouring gel

45g/1½oz/⅓ cup cocoa powder, sifted

2 tbsp/30ml icing/confectioners' sugar

100g/3½oz plain/semisweet chocolate

EQUIPMENT 35 x 25cm/14 x 10in deep baking tin/pan, greased and lined, piping/pastry bag
PREHEAT THE OVEN TO 180°C/350°F/Gas 4

1 To prepare the sponge, whisk together the butter and caster sugar in a bowl using a mixer until light and creamy. Add the eggs and whisk again. Fold in the flour and buttermilk until everything is incorporated. Divide the batter in half between two bowls. To one bowl add the zest of the 2 oranges and a few drops of orange food colouring gel and whisk gently until the batter is an even pale orange colour. Add the sifted cocoa to the other bowl and fold in gently.

2 Spread the chocolate batter in an even layer over the base of the lined tin. Carefully spoon the orange batter on top, small spoonfuls at a time, and spread out on top of the chocolate layer evenly using a spatula. Take care not to move the batter too vigorously as it may mix the layers.

3 Bake in the oven for 20–25 minutes until the cake springs back to your touch and a knife comes out clean when inserted into the centre.

4 Whilst the cake is still warm heat the icing sugar and orange juice in a pan and bring to the boil. Drizzle over the top of the cake and leave to cool.

5 Break the chocolate into pieces and place in a heatproof bowl over a pan of simmering water and simmer until melted. Take care that no water gets into the bowl as this will affect the chocolate. Cut the cake into 24 squares and using a piping bag, pipe spirals of melted chocolate on each square. Use a sharp knife to pull the spirals into spider web shapes and leave to set.

6 As with all cakes, this cake is best eaten on the day it is made but can be stored in an airtight container for up to 2 days.

RED, WHITE AND BLUE
wave-the-flag cake

For patriotic days – be it 4th July, St George's Day, Australia Day or a sporting event – this red, white and blue cake is a perfect celebration. With pretty striped layers and red, white and blue decorations, it is an ideal traybake for street parties.

PREPARATION TIME 20 minutes
BAKING TIME 25–30 minutes
MAKES 24

340g/12oz/2 sticks 6 tbsp butter, margarine or low-fat baking spread

340g/12oz/1½ cups caster/superfine sugar

6 eggs

340g/12oz/2½ cups self-raising/self-rising flour, sifted

2 tbsp/30ml natural/plain low-fat yogurt

1 tsp/5ml vanilla extract

A few drops of red and blue food colouring gel

FOR THE ICING

500g/1¼lb icing/confectioners' sugar

45g/1½oz/3 tbsp butter, softened

75g/2½oz low-fat cream cheese

About 1 tbsp/15ml milk

Red and blue sweets/candies and red liquorice laces

EQUIPMENT 35 x 25cm/14 x 10in deep baking tin/pan, greased and lined
PREHEAT THE OVEN TO 180°C/350°F/Gas 4

1 To prepare the sponge, whisk together the butter and caster sugar in a bowl using a mixer until light and creamy. Add the eggs and whisk again. Fold in the flour, low-fat yogurt and vanilla extract gently. Divide the batter into thirds. Leave one third in the mixing bowl and place the two remaining thirds each in separate bowls. Colour one portion of batter red with a food drops of red food colouring gel and another blue with a few drops of blue food colouring gel.

2 Spread the blue cake batter out over the base of the prepared tin in a thin layer. Place small spoonfuls of the uncoloured cake batter over the blue batter and spread out very gently using a spatula. Work carefully so that you do not mix the layers. Repeat with the third red layer ensuring that all the plain batter is covered.

3 Bake in the oven for 25–30 minutes until the cake is firm to touch and a knife comes out clean when inserted into the centre of the cake. Turn the cake out on to a rack and leave to cool.

4 For the icing, sift the icing sugar into a large mixing bowl. Add the butter, cream cheese and a little milk and whisk until you have a smooth thick icing. If the icing is too stiff add a little more milk. If the icing is too soft add a little more icing sugar.

5 Remove the lining paper from the cake and place on a large serving plate or tray. Spread the icing over the top of the cake and decorate with the sweets and laces. Leave the icing to set and then cut into 24 squares to serve. This cake is best eaten on the day it is made but will store for up to 2 days in an airtight container.

BLACKBERRY
and passion fruit sponge

Blackberry and passion fruit are not a common combination in a cake but you will have to trust me that they are truly delicious together. The tang of the passion fruit curd balances the sweet blackberries perfectly. I love to make this cake in the autumn when there are ripe berries in the hedgerows that are free to pick. Blackberries freeze well so pick plenty and freeze them for cold winter days when you can use them for a treat in crumbles, pies or in this scrumptious traycake.

PREPARATION TIME 15 minutes
BAKING TIME 45–50 minutes
MAKES 24

EQUIPMENT 35 x 25cm/14 x 10in deep baking tin/pan, greased and lined
PREHEAT THE OVEN TO 180°C/350°F/Gas 4

225g/8oz/1 stick 7 tbsp butter, margarine or low-fat baking spread, softened

225g/8oz/1 cup caster/superfine sugar

4 eggs

250g/9oz/scant 2 cups self-raising/self-rising flour, sifted

4 tbsp/60ml passion fruit curd

150g/5oz low-fat natural/plain yogurt

600g/1lb 4oz blackberries

180g/6oz cream cheese

FOR THE CRUMBLE TOPPING

100g/3½oz/¾ cup self-raising/self-rising flour

85g/3oz/⅓ cup caster/superfine sugar

85g/3oz/6 tbsp butter, chilled

1 To prepare the sponge, whisk together the butter and caster sugar in a bowl using a mixer until light and creamy. Add the eggs and whisk again. Whisk in the flour, 2 tablespoons of the passion fruit curd and the yogurt, gently, until everything is incorporated.

2 Spoon the batter into the prepared tin and spread into an even layer using a spatula. Sprinkle the blackberries over the top of the cake mixture evenly.

3 In a separate bowl, whisk together the cream cheese and the remaining 2 tablespoons of the passion fruit curd. Place small spoonfuls of the cream cheese mixture over the top of the cake in between the blackberries.

4 For the crumble topping, sift the flour into a bowl and stir in the sugar. Cut the butter into cubes and rub into the flour mixture with your fingertips until the mixture comes together into large crumbs. Sprinkle the crumbs over the top of the cake and bake in the oven for 45–50 minutes until the cake is firm and springs back to your touch. If the crumble starts to brown too much, cover the top of the cake loosely with a sheet of foil.

5 Allow the cake to cool completely in the tin and then cut into 24 squares. As with all cakes, this cake is best eaten on the day it is made but can be stored in an airtight container in the refrigerator for up to 3 days. It needs to be stored in the refrigerator due to the cream cheese.

LAMINGTONS

Lamingtons are a popular Australian traybake – delicate vanilla sponge coated in a chocolate syrup and rolled in coconut. In a twist on the classic chocolate sauce, I have made a raspberry chocolate sauce which gives these little cakes a lovely flavour.

PREPARATION TIME 30 minutes
BAKING TIME 35–40 minutes
MAKES 20

340g/12oz/2 sticks 6 tbsp butter,
margarine or low-fat baking spread,
softened

340g/12oz/1½ cups caster/superfine
sugar

6 eggs

340g/12oz/2½ cups self-raising/
self-rising flour, sifted

1 tsp/5ml vanilla extract

FOR THE ICING

45g/1½oz butter

300g/10½oz seedless raspberry jam

120g/4oz/1 cup icing/confectioners'
sugar

60g/2oz/½ cup cocoa powder

350g/12½oz desiccated/dry
unsweetened shredded coconut

EQUIPMENT 35 x 25cm/14 x 10in deep baking tin/pan, greased and
lined, cooling rack, foil
PREHEAT THE OVEN TO 180°C/350°F/Gas 4

1 To prepare the sponge, whisk together the butter and caster sugar in a
bowl using a mixer until light and creamy. Add the eggs and whisk again.
Fold in the flour and vanilla extract gently. Spoon the cake batter into the tin
and spread out evenly.

2 Bake in the oven for 35–40 minutes until the cake is firm to touch and a
knife comes out clean when inserted into the centre of the cake. Turn the
bake out on to a cooling rack and leave to cool. Remove the lining paper and
cut the traybake into 20 rectangles.

3 In a pan, heat the butter and raspberry jam with 4 tbsp/60ml of water, then
sift in the icing sugar and cocoa. Whisk together until you have a smooth
syrup. Pass through a sieve or strainer to remove any lumps or seeds and
leave to cool slightly.

4 Place a sheet of foil under a cooling rack to catch any drips of the syrup.
Place the coconut on a large plate or tray. One by one dip the cakes
into the syrup, coating to ensure that all sides of the cake are covered. Roll
the cake in the coconut and transfer to the rack to set. Repeat with all the
remaining cakes.

5 Leave the cakes to set and then serve. These are best eaten on the day they
are made but will store for up to 2 days in an airtight container.

BARS
and Slices

Flapjacks are ideal for fêtes as everyone loves them and they only take around 15 minutes to bake. You can easily make a large batch of the oaty syrup mix and then divide into several bowls and flavour each portion separately – lemon and sultanas, choc chip and cherry are just some of the delicious possibilities. This is a quick way of having a wide variety of differently flavoured bakes to sell with minimum effort.

This chapter also contains all kinds of tempting family favourites such as granola bars, shortcakes and tiffin slices.

Classic bars and slices are perfect for bake sales as they cut easily into portions to serve.

I love the cherry season – rich, juicy and sweet they make a perfect flapjack filling.

When I was young I used to bake Viennese whirls with my Mum.

Granola squares are very moreish and are a good wholesome bake for a cake sale.

Freshly roasted apricots have a sweet sherbet taste.

Rich spiced
fruit in
Pastry layers

NELSON slice

At an archery competition, the judge Pete Mallard told me his favourite cake was a Nelson slice. I had never heard of it! Pete told me that it was like a wedding cake baked between layers of pastry which local bakers used to make – apparently when these slices were put in the shop window they sold out within the hour. This is my version with buttery brioche crumbs, however you can use fresh white breadcrumbs instead.

PREPARATION TIME 45 minutes
BAKING TIME 35–45 minutes
MAKES 24

125g/4½oz/1 stick butter, margarine or low-fat baking spread, softened

115g/4oz/½ cup dark brown sugar

1 tsp/5ml ground cinnamon

1 tsp/5ml ground mixed/apple pie spice

350g/12oz brioche bread

Zest of 1 orange

2 eggs

4 tbsp/60ml brandy or Cointreau

180g/6oz sultanas/golden raisins

180g/6oz currants

1 tbsp/15ml icing/confectioners' sugar, sifted, plus extra for dusting

FOR THE SHORTCRUST PASTRY

350g/12oz/2¼ cups plain/all-purpose flour, plus extra for dusting

Pinch of salt

175g/6oz/1½ sticks butter, chilled and cut into cubes

EQUIPMENT food processor, rolling pin, 35 x 25cm/14 x 10in deep baking tin/pan, greased and lined, pastry brush
PREHEAT THE OVEN TO 180°C/350°F/Gas 4

1 To make the pastry, place the flour and salt in a large mixing bowl and rub the butter into the flour with your fingertips to form fine breadcrumbs. Add 2–3 tbsp/30–45ml chilled water, a little at a time, mixing with a flat-bladed knife until you have a soft dough. Bring the dough together in a ball with your hands and wrap in baking parchment, cling film or plastic wrap. Chill in the refrigerator for at least 30 minutes while you prepare the filling. (If you do not have time to make your own pastry you can use a readymade 500g/1¼lb block of shortcrust pastry instead. This is available in most supermarkets and comes in regular or sweet varieties. You can use either in this recipe.)

2 Whisk together the butter and brown sugar with the ground cinnamon and ground mixed spice. Blitz the brioche in a food processor to fine crumbs. Add the crumbs to the butter mixture with the orange zest, one of the eggs and the brandy or Cointreau, and whisk in. Add the sultanas and currants and fold in.

3 On a clean flour-dusted surface, cut the pastry in half and roll out one half thinly to the size of your tin using a rolling pin. Cut into a neat rectangle the size of your tin and carefully lift into the lined tin. Patch any cracks or gaps with the pastry trimmings to ensure that you have completely covered the base with pastry. Beat the second egg and brush a thin layer of the egg over the pastry to seal it using the pastry brush.

4 Spread the fruit mixture over the pastry in an even layer, pressing it down on to the pastry. Roll out the second half of pastry into the same size rectangle following the instructions above and then lift carefully on top of the fruit layer. Again patch any gaps with pastry trimmings. Score a decorative pattern into the pastry with a sharp knife, taking care not to cut all the way through.

5 Whisk the icing sugar into the remaining beaten egg and then brush over the top of the pastry to glaze. You can use any spare pastry trimmings to cut into pretty patterns and flowers if you wish, glazing before you bake. Bake in the oven for 35–45 minutes until the pastry is crisp and golden brown on top. Leave to cool in the tin, then remove and cut into 24 squares and dust with icing sugar to serve. This slice will store for up to 3 days.

CHOCOLATE CHIP flapjack

This is a rich and indulgent flapjack filled with deep cocoa flavours and topped with delicious chocolate chips. For an extra-indulgent treat you can add white chocolate chips or peanut butter chips as well, or even stir additional chips into the flapjack mixture before baking.

PREPARATION TIME 10 minutes
BAKING TIME 15–20 minutes
MAKES 24

250g/9oz/2 sticks butter, margarine or low-fat baking spread

250g/9oz/1¼ cups dark brown sugar

6 tbsp/90ml golden/light corn syrup

500g/1¼lb/5 cups porridge/rolled oats

60g/2oz/½ cup cocoa powder, sifted

2 tsp/10ml vanilla extract

A pinch of salt

200g/7oz plain/semisweet chocolate chips

EQUIPMENT 35 x 25cm/14 x 10in deep baking tin/pan, greased and lined
PREHEAT THE OVEN TO 180°C/350°F/Gas 4

1 Place the butter, dark brown sugar and syrup in a large heavy pan and simmer over a gentle heat until the butter and sugar have melted. Add the oats, cocoa, vanilla and salt to the pan and stir well so that all the oats are coated and the cocoa powder is mixed in.

2 Tip the mixture into the lined pan and spread out in an even layer using a spatula or the back of a large spoon.

3 Bake in the oven for 15–20 minutes until the top of the flapjack is just firm. Remove from the oven, leave to cool for about 5 minutes then sprinkle the chocolate chips over the top of the flapjack. The warmth of the flapjack will allow the chips to melt slightly. Leave to cool completely.

4 When cool remove the lining and cut the flapjack into 24 squares and store in an airtight container until needed. The flapjack will store for at least 5 days.

Hint and tip

For a peanut butter and white chocolate version, omit the cocoa and add 2 tbsp/30ml of crunchy peanut butter with the oats. Replace the plain/semisweet chocolate chips with white chocolate chips or chopped white chocolate.

CHERRY COMPOTE
flapjacks

I love the cherry season – rich, juicy and sweet they make a perfect pudding just served in a large bowl on their own. But when I have a large cherry harvest (and manage to beat the birds to picking the cherries) I love to make compote to store for later in the year when the weather is a little gloomy and I need a taste of summer to pick me up. Supermarkets sell good cherry compote that you can use for this recipe, or alternatively you can use a can of cherry pie filling for equally delicious results.

Hint and tip
For a healthier alternative replace the butter with low-fat baking spread. If you wish you can replace the vanilla with a little almond extract which will also go well with the cherries.

PREPARATION TIME 10 minutes
BAKING TIME 15–20 minutes
MAKES 24

EQUIPMENT 35 x 25cm/14 x 10in deep baking tin/pan, greased and lined
PREHEAT THE OVEN TO 180°C/350°F/Gas 4

250g/9oz/2 sticks butter or margarine

6 tbsp/90ml golden/light corn syrup

250g/9oz/1¼ cups caster/superfine sugar

Seeds of 1 vanilla pod/bean

500g/1¼lb/5 cups porridge/rolled oats

150g/5oz dried cherries

A pinch of salt

400g/14oz/1 heaped cup cherry compote

1 Place the butter, syrup and caster sugar in a large heavy pan and simmer over a gentle heat until the butter and sugar have melted. Add the vanilla seeds, oats, dried cherries and salt to the pan and stir well so that all the oats are coated in the syrup.

2 Tip half of the oat mixture into the lined pan and spread out in an even layer using a spatula or the back of a large spoon. Spoon over the cherry compote in an even layer. If the cherry compote is very runny, remove some of the liquid as it will make the flapjack soggy.

3 Top the cherries with the remaining flapjack mixture and spread out into a layer so that all of the cherry compote is covered.

4 Bake in the oven for 15–20 minutes until the top of the flapjack is golden brown. Remove from the oven and leave to cool completely. When cool remove the lining paper and cut the flapjack into 24 squares. Store in an airtight container until needed. The flapjack will store for at least 5 days.

DOUBLE-GINGER
flapjack

I love the tangy flavour of ginger, and this gorgeous flapjack contains two types of ginger – ground ginger for a peppery flavour and stem ginger preserved in syrup for a sweet crunch in the flapjack. Why not serve it with ginger tea – simply place a few slices of fresh peeled root ginger steeped in hot water and leave for a few minutes to infuse. Delicious!

PREPARATION TIME 10 minutes
BAKING TIME 15–20 minutes
MAKES 24

250g/9oz/2 sticks butter or margarine

6 tbsp/90ml golden/light corn syrup

250g/9oz/1¼ cups caster/superfine sugar

8 balls of preserved stem ginger

2 tsp/10ml ground ginger

500g/1¼lb/5 cups porridge/rolled oats

A pinch of salt

EQUIPMENT 35 x 25cm/14 x 10in deep baking tin/pan, greased and lined
PREHEAT THE OVEN TO 180°C/350°F/Gas 4

1 Place the butter, syrup and sugar in a large heavy pan and simmer over a gentle heat until the butter and sugar have melted. Finely chop the ginger using a sharp knife. Add the ground ginger, oats, salt and chopped preserved ginger to the pan and stir well so that all the oats are coated in the syrup.

2 Tip the oats into the lined pan and spread out in an even layer using a spatula or the back of a large spoon.

3 Bake in the oven for 15–20 minutes until the top of the flapjack is golden brown. Remove from the oven and leave to cool completely. When cool remove the lining paper and cut the flapjack into 24 squares. Store in an airtight container until needed. The flapjacks will store for at least 5 days.

Hint and tip
For a healthier alternative replace the butter with low-fat baking spread.

LEMON AND SULTANA
flapjack

This is a classic flapjack and is always popular, with large juicy sultanas and the zesty tang of lemon. You can easily vary the flavour of this recipe with other citrus flavours and fruit – why not try orange and cranberry or lime and cherry? This is one of my favourite treats for a pack-up lunch as the flapjack is rich and gooey and travels well.

PREPARATION TIME 10 minutes
BAKING TIME 15–20 minutes
MAKES 24

BARS AND SLICES

250g/9oz/2 sticks butter, margarine or low-fat baking spread

6 tbsp/90ml golden/light corn syrup

250g/9oz/1¼ cups dark brown sugar

Zest of 2 unwaxed lemons

500g/1¼lb/5 cups porridge/rolled oats

200g/7oz sultanas/golden raisins

A pinch of salt

EQUIPMENT 35 x 25cm/14 x 10in deep baking tin-pan, greased and lined
PREHEAT THE OVEN TO 180°C/350°F/Gas 4

1 Place the butter, syrup and dark brown sugar in a large heavy pan and simmer over a gentle heat until the butter and sugar have melted. Add the lemon zest, oats, sultanas and salt to the pan and stir well so that all the oats are coated in the syrup.

2 Tip the mixture into the lined pan and spread out in an even layer using a spatula or the back of a large spoon.

3 Bake in the oven for 15–20 minutes until the top of the flapjack is golden brown. Remove from the oven and leave to cool completely. When cool remove the lining paper and cut the flapjack into 24 squares. Store in an airtight container until needed. The flapjack will store for at least 5 days.

GRANOLA squares

These squares are great for packed lunches and picnics as they travel well and are very moreish, full of dried apples, dates and cranberries. They are also a good wholesome bake for a cake sale. You can vary the flavour by adding different fruits if you wish – dried cherries and blueberries are yummy and you can add extra crunch with a handful of nuts such as pecans or walnuts.

Hint and tip
If you have lots of apples in your garden, peel and core them and slice thinly. Coat in a little lemon juice to stop them browning and bake in the oven on a very low setting until they have dried and are chewy. Store in an airtight container until you need them.

PREPARATION TIME 20 minutes
BAKING TIME 20–30 minutes
MAKES 24

BARS AND SLICES

200g/7oz/1 stick and 5 tbsp butter, margarine or low-fat baking spread

2 tbsp/30ml golden/light corn syrup

300g/10oz/2 cups plain/all-purpose flour

300g/10oz granola

115g/4oz/½ cup caster/superfine sugar

150g/5oz dried cranberries

100g/3½oz dried apple rings, chopped into small pieces

100g/3½oz dates, chopped into small pieces

EQUIPMENT 35 x 25cm/14 x 10in deep baking tin/pan, greased and lined
PREHEAT THE OVEN TO 180°C/350°F/Gas 4

1 Place the butter and syrup in a pan and simmer over a gentle heat until the butter has melted.

2 Sift the flour into a large mixing bowl and stir in the granola, sugar, cranberries, chopped apple and chopped dates.

3 Pour in the butter and syrup mixture and stir so that the mixture becomes soft and forms a dough, if you don't mind getting messy you can use your hands here. Press out into the lined tin.

4 Bake in the oven for 20–30 minutes until lightly golden brown then leave to cool in the tin. Remove the lining paper and cut into 24 squares to serve. This traybake will store for up to 5 days in an airtight container.

OATY APRICOT
slice

I love oats, and whilst flapjack is one of the things I like to bake most, this oaty slice is more delicate and light but still with the same oaty goodness. If you are short of time you can replace the fresh apricots with about 30 dried apricots, but I find freshly roasted apricots have a sweet sherbet taste and make this slice so much nicer, so do try and roast them if you can – it will be worth the effort. This slice keeps well and is perfect for picnics and lunchboxes.

PREPARATION TIME 30 minutes
BAKING TIME 1 hour 30 minutes
MAKES 30

450g/1lb fresh apricots

200g/7oz/1 stick and 5 tbsp butter, margarine or low-fat baking spread

340g/12oz/3¼ cups plain/all-purpose flour, sifted

225g/8oz porridge/rolled oats

180g/6oz/scant 1 cup caster/superfine sugar

2 tbsp/30ml golden/light corn syrup

1 egg, beaten

Zest of 1 lemon

EQUIPMENT roasting dish, 35 x 25cm/14 x 10in deep baking tin/pan, greased and lined, cake cases
PREHEAT THE OVEN TO 140°C/275°F/Gas 1

1 Cut the apricots in half and remove the stones/pits. Lay the apricots in a roasting dish, cut side up and bake in the oven for about an hour until the fruit is soft. Leave to cool.

2 Turn the oven temperature up to 180°C/350°F/Gas 4. Melt the butter in a pan and leave to cool. Place the flour, oats and sugar in a mixing bowl and stir together to mix everything. Pour in the cooled melted butter, golden syrup and the beaten egg and whisk in. The dough should be loose and crumbly but should hold together when you press it with your fingers.

3 Spoon just over half of the mixture into the prepared tin and press down flat with your clean fingertips so that the whole base is covered.

4 Roughly chop the cooled apricots into small pieces and mix with the lemon zest. Sprinkle over the oaty base mixture so that the apricots are evenly distributed.

5 Sprinkle the remaining oat mixture on top of the apricots and press down. Bake for 25–30 minutes until the top of the slice is golden brown. Leave to cool in the tin then cut into 24 slices to serve. This slice will keep for up to 3 days stored in an airtight container.

APPLE shortcake

When I was young I used to bake Viennese whirls with my mum. Delicious buttery pastry swirls, sweetened with icing sugar and decorated with a little homemade jam. I have used a Viennese pastry as the base of this apple shortbread-style traybake. With a delectable sweet apple layer and a buttery crumble top, it is sure to be popular at fêtes and fairs.

Hint and tip
If you have a glut of pears or quinces, make pear or quince purée in the same way as the apple for equally delicious results.

PREPARATION TIME 20 minutes
BAKING TIME 25–30 minutes
MAKES 24

EQUIPMENT 35 x 25cm/14 x 10in deep baking tin/pan, greased and lined
PREHEAT THE OVEN TO 180°C/350°F/Gas 4

1kg/2¼lb cooking apples, peeled and cored

100g/3½oz/½ cup caster/superfine sugar

1 tsp/5ml ground cinnamon

250g/9oz/2 sticks butter, margarine or low-fat baking spread, softened

100g/3½oz/scant 1 cup icing/confectioners' sugar, sifted

250g/9oz/generous 1¾ cups plain/all-purpose flour, sifted, plus extra for dusting

FOR THE CRUMBLE TOPPING

140g/5oz/1 cup self-raising/self-rising flour

85g/3oz/⅓ cup caster/superfine sugar

1 tsp/5ml vanilla extract

100g/3½oz/7 tbsp butter, chilled

1 Chop the peeled apples into small pieces and place in a pan over a gentle heat with the caster sugar, ground cinnamon and 5 tbsp/75ml of water. Simmer until the apple is soft. If the water evaporates before the apple is soft add a little more water to the pan. Leave to cool completely.

2 Cream together butter and icing sugar until light and creamy. Whisk in the sifted flour to make a soft dough. Dust your hands with flour and then press the soft dough out into the lined tin in an even layer. Chill in the refrigerator for 30 minutes.

3 For the crumble topping, sift the flour into a bowl and stir in the sugar and vanilla. Cut the chilled butter into cubes and rub into the flour with your fingertips until the mixtures resembles large breadcrumbs.

4 Spread the cooled apple over the shortbread base and then sprinkle over the crumble in a thin layer. Bake for 25–30 minutes until the crumble is golden brown. Leave to cool completely in the tin, then cut into 24 squares to serve. This slice will store for up to 3 days in an airtight container.

CRISPY TIFFIN slice

This delicious and indulgent no-bake slice is a combination of two of my favourite things – crispy cakes and chocolate tiffin. You can vary the flavour of the tiffin by using different types of biscuits and a variety of dried fruits. Try Oreo cookies with dried cranberries and a little orange zest for a winter version of this yummy treat!

PREPARATION TIME 20 minutes
COOKING TIME 10 minutes
MAKES 24

340g/11⅓oz marshmallows

125g/4½oz/1 stick butter

180g/6oz/3–4 cups rice crispies

100g/3½oz white chocolate, for decorating

FOR THE TIFFIN LAYER

300g/10½oz plain/semisweet chocolate

125g/4½oz/1 stick butter

2 tbsp/30ml golden/light corn syrup

200g/7oz custard cream biscuits or other sandwich cookies

125g/4½oz raisins

EQUIPMENT 35 x 25cm/14 x 10in deep baking tin/pan, greased and lined

1 In a large heavy pan, melt the marshmallows and butter over a gentle heat, stirring all the time so that the marshmallows do not burn. The mixture will become very gooey. Working quickly so that the mixture does not cool, stir in the rice crispies well so that they are all coated.

2 Place the crispies into the base of the lined tin and press out into an even layer using a spatula or the back of a spoon. Leave to set.

3 For the tiffin layer, break the plain chocolate into squares and place in a heatproof bowl with the butter and golden syrup and place over a pan of simmering water. Simmer until the chocolate melts and the mixture becomes smooth and glossy, stirring occasionally.

4 Break the biscuits into small pieces and stir into the chocolate mixture with the raisins. Spoon the mixture into the tin on top of the marshmallow layer. Chill in the refrigerator for several hours until the tiffin has set.

5 Break the white chocolate into pieces and place in a heatproof bowl over a pan of simmering water. Simmer until the chocolate has melted then spoon in large drizzles over the top of the slice swirled in pretty patterns. The chocolate should set quickly on the cold tiffin; if not, return to the refrigerator to set for a little longer.

6 Remove the lining paper and cut the tiffin into 24 squares using a sharp knife and serve. This cake will store for up to 5 days in the refrigerator.

BROWNIES
and Blondies

These are ideal traybakes for a bake sale as they last well and can therefore be made a few days in advance, allowing you more time for baking cakes nearer the day. There are so many variations possible with brownies and blondies and once you have mastered the basic method you can adapt the recipes to include all your favourite flavours.

This chapter contains some delicious cherry brownies (which are gluten-free although you wouldn't know it) as well as chocolate peppermint brownies. Yum!

Brownies and blondies are rich and indulgent and loved by all.

Pistachio nuts make blondies look pretty and they are sure to sell fast at your bake sale.

To me, Christmas would not be Christmas without peppermint bark!

S'mores are the perfect campfire treat – gooey toasted marshmallows, here on a traybake!

CHOCOLATE
and cherry brownies

My friend Lucy cannot eat wheat, so she loves these brownies. They are so delicious that no one would know they are gluten-free. Regular plain flour is substituted with gluten-free plain or all-purpose flour although if you do not need the brownies to be gluten-free you can just use regular flour instead. Using ready-made cherry compote saves time and it is available in supermarkets but if you cannot find any, a can of cherry pie filling will work well too.

PREPARATION TIME 15 minutes
BAKING TIME 25–30 minutes
MAKES 24

300g/10oz plain/semisweet chocolate, gluten-free

250g/9oz/2 sticks butter, margarine or low-fat baking spread

200g/7oz/1 cup caster/superfine sugar

200g/7oz/scant 1 cup dark brown sugar

5 large/US extra large eggs

200g/7oz/1½ cups gluten-free plain/all-purpose flour, sifted

150g/5oz dried cherries

400g/14oz/2 cups cherry compote

EQUIPMENT 35 x 25cm/14 x 10in deep baking tin/pan, greased and lined
PREHEAT THE OVEN TO 180°C/350°F/Gas 4

1 Break the chocolate into small pieces and place in a heatproof bowl with the butter over a pan of simmering water and heat until the chocolate and butter have melted and you have a smooth glossy sauce. Remove from the heat and leave to cool whilst you make the brownie mixture. If you are short of time you can place the broken chocolate and butter in a microwaveproof bowl and microwave on high power for about 1–2 minutes, stirring part-way through.

2 For the brownies, whisk the caster sugar and dark brown sugar with the eggs using a mixer or a whisk, until the mixture is very light and creamy and has doubled in size. Whilst still whisking, slowly pour in the melted chocolate and butter mixture.

3 Fold in the gluten-free flour, then stir in the dried cherries. Pour half of the mixture into the prepared tin and spread out in an even layer.

4 Using a spoon, gently place spoonfuls of the cherry compote over the brownie mixture evenly. Pour over the remaining brownie mixture. It is best to do this very slowly so that all the cherry compote is covered.

5 Bake in the oven for 25–30 minutes until a crust has formed on top of the brownies but they still feel a little soft underneath. Allow to cool completely before removing the lining paper and cutting into 24 squares. These brownies will store in an airtight container for at least 3 days.

Hint and tip

Make sure that the dried cherries you use are gluten-free and do not contain a wheat-based anti-caking agent.

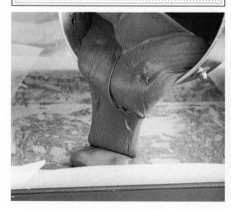

S'MORES brownies

S'mores are the perfect campfire treat – toasted marshmallows sandwiched between graham crackers with chunks of chocolate. The warmth of the toasted marshmallows starts to melt the chocolate, giving you one utterly delicious treat. I have taken all the elements of the classic s'more and incorporated them into these indulgent brownies.

PREPARATION TIME 20 minutes
BAKING TIME 25–30 minutes
MAKES 24

150g/5oz/1 stick 2 tbsp butter, margarine or low-fat baking spread

225g/8oz plain/semisweet chocolate

250g/9oz/scant 2 cups caster/ superfine sugar

3 eggs

1 tsp/5ml vanilla salt, or a pinch of salt and 1 tsp/5ml vanilla extract

130g/4½oz plain/all-purpose flour, sifted

200g/7oz marshmallow fluff

FOR THE BISCUIT BASE

300g/10½oz digestive biscuits/ graham crackers

150g/5oz/1 stick 2 tbsp butter, margarine or low-fat baking spread

EQUIPMENT food processor, 35 x 25cm/14 x 10in deep baking tin/pan, greased and lined, chef's blow torch
PREHEAT THE OVEN TO 180°C/350°F/Gas 4

1 Start by preparing the biscuit base. Crush the digestives to very fine crumbs in a food processor or blender or bash in a clean plastic bag with a rolling pin. Melt the butter in a pan over a gentle heat, taking care that the butter does not brown. Stir the melted butter into the biscuit crumbs and mix well. Place the crumbs into the tin and press down firmly using the back of a small spoon.

2 To prepare the brownies, melt the butter and plain chocolate in a heatproof bowl resting over a small pan of simmering water, taking care that the bottom of the bowl does not touch the water and stir until melted. Leave aside to cool.

3 Whisk the caster sugar with the eggs and vanilla salt in a large bowl using a mixer or a whisk until the mixture is very light and has doubled in size. Whilst still whisking, slowly pour in the cooled melted chocolate mixture.

4 Fold in the flour using a spatula and pour the batter into the prepared tin on top of the biscuit base. Bake for about 25–30 minutes until the brownies have formed a crust and a knife comes out clean with no cake batter on it when inserted into the middle of the pan. Allow to cool.

5 When you are ready to serve, cut the brownies into 24 squares. Spoon a little marshmallow fluff on to each square and caramelize with the blow torch. The brownies will store for up to 3 days in an airtight container – decorate with the marshmallow fluff just before serving.

PEPPERMINT
brownies

with 'peppermint bark' topping

I was introduced to the delights of peppermint bark by my American friend Martha Murphey. For those of you who have not discovered this festive treat, it is white chocolate flavoured with peppermint extract set in a sheet with finely chopped peppermint candy canes on top. To me, Christmas would not be Christmas without peppermint bark! This brownie traybake is inspired by this delicious sweet – flavoured with peppermint chocolate and peppermint extract, and topped with candy canes and white chocolate.

PREPARATION TIME 20 minutes
BAKING TIMEA 25–30 minutes
MAKES 24

200g/7oz plain/semisweet chocolate

200g/7oz mint chocolate

250g/9oz/2 sticks butter, margarine or low-fat baking spread

150g/5oz/¾ cup caster/superfine sugar

150g/5oz/generous ½ cup dark brown sugar

5 large/US extra large eggs

1 tsp/5ml peppermint extract

A pinch of vanilla salt or a pinch of salt and 1 tsp/5ml vanilla extract

200g/7oz/1½ cups plain/all-purpose flour, sifted

100g/3½oz mint chocolate sticks

100g/3½oz white chocolate

2–3 peppermint candy canes

EQUIPMENT 35 x 25cm/14 x 10in deep baking tin/pan, greased and lined, rolling pin
PREHEAT THE OVEN TO 180°C/350°F/Gas 4

1 Break the plain and mint chocolate into small pieces and place in a heatproof bowl with the butter over a pan of simmering water, making sure that the bottom of the bowl does not touch the water. Heat until the chocolate and butter have melted and you have smooth glossy sauce. If you are short of time you can melt the broken chocolate and butter in a microwaveproof bowl and microwave on high power for 1–2 minutes, stirring part-way through.

2 Remove the melted chocolate from the heat, or the microwave, and leave to cool whilst you make the brownie mixture. Whisk the caster sugar and dark brown sugar with the eggs using a mixer or a whisk until the mixture is very light and creamy and has doubled in size.

3 Whisk in the peppermint extract and vanilla salt (or regular salt and vanilla). Whilst still whisking, slowly pour in the cooled melted chocolate and butter mixture. Fold in the flour. Chop the mint chocolate sticks into small pieces and stir in.

4 Pour the mixture into the prepared tin and spread out in an even layer. Bake in the oven for 25–30 minutes until a crust has formed on top of the brownies but they still feel a little soft underneath. Remove from the oven and leave to cool.

5 Place the white chocolate, broken into pieces, in a heatproof bowl over a pan of simmering water and heat until the chocolate has melted. Drizzle the chocolate in pretty patterns over the top of the brownie using a whisk.

6 Crush the candy canes into pieces by placing them in a clean food bag and bashing with a rolling pin. Sprinkle over the melted chocolate and leave to set. Cut the brownies into 24 squares. They will store in an airtight container for up to 3 days.

Yummy healthier version

SKINNY BANOFFEE brownies

Brownies are often calorie-laden and filled with chocolate and butter – it's what makes them so delicious! They are not ideal though if you are watching your weight. These brownies are made with cocoa rather than chocolate and have added natural sweetness from the bananas so they are a good skinny alternative and still taste sumptuous even with half of the sugar of normal brownies. If you want a special (non-diet) treat, sprinkle the top of the brownie with mini fudge pieces but this is strictly optional!

PREPARATION TIME 20 minutes
BAKING TIME 25–30 minutes
MAKES 24

200g/7oz/1 stick and 5 tbsp low-fat baking spread, softened

200g/7oz/scant 1 cup dark brown sugar

5 eggs

180g/6oz/1¼ cup plain/all-purpose flour

60g/2oz/½ cup cocoa powder

1 tsp/5ml ground cinnamon

3 ripe bananas

60g/2oz mini fudge pieces (optional)

Juice of 1 lemon

EQUIPMENT 35 x 25cm/14 x 10in deep baking tin/pan, greased and lined
PREHEAT THE OVEN TO 180°C/350°F/Gas 4

1 Melt the low-fat baking spread in a pan and leave to cool. Place the sugar and eggs in a mixing bowl and whisk the mixture until light and creamy. This should take about 5 minutes. Whisk in the melted spread.

2 Sift in the flour, cocoa and cinnamon and fold in gently. Peel 2 of the bananas and crush with a fork until you have a smooth purée. Fold into the brownie mixture.

3 Pour the mixture into the prepared tin. Sprinkle with the fudge pieces, if using. Peel the remaining banana and cut into thin slices. Coat lightly in the lemon juice to prevent it discolouring and distribute the slices over the top of the brownie.

4 Bake in the oven for 25–30 minutes until a crust has formed on top and the brownie is still soft underneath. Leave to cool completely in the tin then cut into 24 slices to serve. These brownies will store for up to 2 days in an airtight container but are best eaten on the day they are made.

PECAN PIE
blondies

I love the classic American favourite of pecan pie with its buttery pastry case and delicious flavours of cinnamon and vanilla, all wrapped up in nutty pecans. This is my blondie version with a white chocolate traybake topped with pecans and then brushed with a light spiced pecan pie glaze. Fantastic!

PREPARATION TIME 20 minutes
BAKING TIME 25–30 minutes
MAKES 24

350g/12½oz white chocolate

250g/9oz/2 sticks butter, margarine or low-fat baking spread

5 eggs

300g/10½oz/1¼ cups caster/superfine sugar

1 tsp/5ml vanilla extract

A pinch of vanilla salt or regular salt

200g/7oz/1½ cups plain/all-purpose flour

2 tsp/10ml ground cinnamon

200g/7oz/generous 1½ cups pecan halves

FOR THE GLAZE

1 tbsp/15ml dark brown sugar

50g/1¾oz butter

2tbsp/30ml golden/light corn syrup

1 tsp/5ml vanilla extract

1 tsp/5ml ground cinnamon

EQUIPMENT 35 x 25cm/14 x 10in deep baking tin/pan, greased and lined, pastry brush
PREHEAT THE OVEN TO 180°C/350°F/Gas 4

1 Place the white chocolate and butter in a heatproof bowl resting over a pan of simmering water and stir until melted. Take care that no water gets into the bowl. Leave to cool slightly.

2 Whisk together the eggs and caster sugar using an electric whisk until the mixture is thick and creamy and has doubled in size. Add the chocolate mixture and whisk in. Add the vanilla extract and vanilla salt. Sift in the flour and ground cinnamon and fold in gently.

3 Pour the mixture into the prepared tin. Sprinkle the top of the blondie with the pecans.

4 Bake for 25–30 minutes until the top of the blondie has a crust on top and the blondie feels fairly firm but still slightly soft underneath. Leave to cool.

5 For the glaze, place the sugar, butter, golden syrup, vanilla and cinnamon in a pan and simmer until the butter and sugar have melted. Remove from the heat and leave to cool for a few minutes then brush the top of the blondie with the glaze using a pastry brush.

6 When cool, remove the lining paper, cut the blondie into 24 slices and store in an airtight container for up to 5 days.

PISTACHIO
and white chocolate blondie

Pistachios are a vibrant nut and have such a wonderful flavour that they make a rich and indulgent traybake. I love to sprinkle chopped white chocolate and pistachio nuts on top to make these blondies look super-pretty which should ensure that they sell fast at your bake sale.

PREPARATION TIME 20 minutes
BAKING TIME 25–30 minutes
MAKES 24

200g/7oz/2 cups pistachio nuts

4 tbsp/60ml sunflower or other flavourless oil

2 tbsp/30ml icing/confectioners' sugar

250g/9oz/2 sticks butter, margarine or low-fat baking spread

4 eggs

400g/14oz/1¾ cups caster/superfine sugar

250g/9oz/generous 1¾ cups plain/all-purpose flour

250g/9oz white chocolate, chopped

EQUIPMENT food processor, 35 x 25cm/14 x 10in deep baking tin/pan, greased and lined
PREHEAT THE OVEN TO 180°C/350°F/Gas 4

1 Blitz the pistachio nuts to fine crumbs in a food processor and reserve a few tablespoons for the top of the blondies. Add the oil and icing sugar to the remaining pistachio nuts and blitz to a smooth paste. Melt the butter in a pan and leave to cool.

2 Whisk together the eggs and caster sugar. Stir the pistachio paste into the melted butter and add to the egg mixture and whisk well until incorporated. Sift in the flour and whisk in gently until just incorporated. Pour into the lined tin. Sprinkle the chopped chocolate over the top and the reserved chopped pistachio nuts.

3 Bake for 25–30 minutes until a crust has formed on top but the blondie is still soft underneath. Leave to cool in the tin completely. When you are ready to serve, remove the lining paper and cut the blondie into 24 squares. These blondies will store well for up to 3 days in an airtight container.

Hint and tip
For best results use bright green pistachios – Iranian and Turkish supermarkets usually have a good choice. You can substitute other nuts in place of the pistachios such as hazelnuts or walnuts if you prefer.

RASPBERRY CHEESECAKE
blondies

Everyone loves raspberry cheesecake. These blondies – creamy with white chocolate – have a cheesecake layer and fresh berries and for extra crunch are topped with a sprinkling of biscuit crumbs.

PREPARATION TIME 10 minutes
BAKING TIME 30–40 minutes
MAKES 24

250g/9oz/2 sticks butter, margarine or low-fat baking spread

250g/9oz white chocolate, chopped

4 eggs

250g/9oz/scant 2 cups caster/ superfine sugar

100g/3½oz/½ cup dark brown sugar

A pinch of salt

1 tsp/5ml vanilla extract

250g/9oz/generous 1¾ cups plain/ all-purpose flour, sifted

FOR THE CHEESECAKE MIXTURE

300g/10½oz low-fat cream cheese

2 tbsp/30ml icing/confectioners' sugar, sifted

2 egg yolks

400g/14oz raspberries

3 digestive biscuits/graham crackers

EQUIPMENT 35 x 25cm/14 x 10in deep baking tin/pan, greased and lined
PREHEAT THE OVEN TO 180°C/350°F/Gas 4

1 Melt the butter in a pan over a gentle heat. Remove from the heat and add the white chocolate to the warm butter and stir occasionally, so that the white chocolate melts.

2 Whisk together the eggs and the caster sugar and brown sugar with the salt and vanilla until the mixture is thick and creamy and the mixture has doubled in size. Fold in the flour and the chocolate mixture and then pour the batter into the prepared tin.

3 In a separate bowl, whisk together the cream cheese, icing sugar and egg yolks until smooth. Sprinkle the raspberries over the top of the blondie mixture and then place spoonfuls of the cream cheese mixture between the raspberries.

4 Crush the digestives into small pieces with your hands and sprinkle over the raspberries and cream cheese. Bake for 30–40 minutes, then remove from the oven and leave to cool in the tin completely.

5 Remove the lining paper and cut the blondies into 24 squares to serve. Store in an airtight container for up to 3 days.

Hint and tip

For a blueberry cheesecake version, replace the raspberries with fresh blueberries. Blackberries and pitted cherries also work well.

COCONUT
blondie brownies

This recipe was created with me by a wonderful little baker Charlotte Faulkner – her favourite programme is the Great British Bake Off and she just loves to bake. Although these brownies are gluten-free they are unctuous and gooey and can be served to everyone. They have a pretty stripy effect with both a blondie and brownie layer although if you prefer you can just make them with plain chocolate.

PREPARATION TIME 20 minutes
BAKING TIME 25–30 minutes
MAKES 24

200g/7oz plain/semisweet chocolate

250g/9oz/2 sticks butter, margarine or low-fat baking spread

200g/7oz white chocolate

5 eggs

400g/14oz/1¾ cups caster/superfine sugar

200g/7oz/2⅔ cups soft shredded coconut (such as Angel Flake)

200g/7oz/1½ cups gluten-free plain/all-purpose flour, sifted

EQUIPMENT 35 x 25cm/14 x 10in deep baking tin/pan, greased and lined
PREHEAT THE OVEN TO 180°C/350°F/Gas 4

1 Break the plain chocolate into small pieces and place in a heatproof bowl with half of the butter over a pan of simmering water and heat until the chocolate and butter have melted and you have a smooth glossy sauce.

2 Do the same with the white chocolate and remaining butter so that you have both a melted white chocolate mixture and a plain chocolate mixture. Remove both mixtures from the heat and leave to cool whilst you make the brownie mixture.

3 Whisk together the eggs and caster sugar for around 5 minutes until the mixture is very light and creamy and has doubled in size. Divide into two mixing bowls and fold the white chocolate mixture into one and the plain chocolate mixture into the other with a spatula. Fold half of the coconut and flour into each bowl so that everything is incorporated.

4 Pour the plain chocolate batter into the prepared tin and spread out in an even layer. Pour the white chocolate mixture on top, taking care that the two layers do not mix.

5 Bake in the oven for 25–30 minutes until a crust has formed on top but the blondie brownies still feel a little soft underneath. Leave to cool in the tin and then remove the lining paper and cut into 24 squares to serve. This brownie will store well for up to 3 days in an airtight container.

Hint and tip
If you do not have soft shredded coconut use desiccated/dry unsweetened shredded coconut instead.

LAYER
Traybakes

This chapter contains the prettiest of traybakes, with delicate layers that will look elegant on any cake stand. There is a millionaire's shortbread with a twist of chocolate shortcake on the base and a white chocolate topping and also one of my school favourites, a coconut mint slice with dark chocolate layers and a white peppermint cream. For more fruity flavours there is a raspberry layer tart topped with syrupy cornflakes and a strawberry crumble slice with a delicious crunch of pine nuts.

This chapter includes possibly the most scrumptious trabake of all – the seven-layer caramel nut bar – I urge you to try it!

Cherries and chocolate are always a winning combination.

Millionaire's shortbread is one of the ultimate treats.

A light lemon macaron filling topped with crushed meringue. Yum, yum!

The smell of sweet strawberries from the oven will get your tastebuds tingling.

UPSIDE-DOWN Millionaire's shortbread

Millionaire's shortbread is one of the ultimate treats – a buttery shortbread base topped with a thick caramel and chocolate topping. This is my reversed version with a chocolate shortbread base and a white chocolate topping in place of the traditional milk chocolate. It is rich and indulgent so cut the squares small to serve.

PREPARATION TIME 30 minutes
BAKING TIME 10–15 minutes
MAKES 30

300g/10oz/2 cups plain/all-purpose flour

85g/3oz/¾ cup cocoa powder

60g/2oz/¼ cup caster/superfine sugar

180g/6oz/1½ sticks butter, margarine or low-fat baking spread

1–2 tbsp/15–30ml milk

250g/9oz white chocolate

FOR THE CARAMEL LAYER

125g/4½oz/⅔ cup dark brown sugar

125g/4½oz/1 stick butter

600g/1lb 6oz condensed milk

Pinch of salt

EQUIPMENT 35 x 25cm/14 x 10in deep baking tin/pan, greased and lined
PREHEAT THE OVEN TO 180°C/350°F/Gas 4

1 Sift the flour into a bowl with the cocoa. Stir in the sugar. Rub the butter in with your fingertips until it is all incorporated. Add the milk and bring the dough together with your hands. You may not need all of the milk so add it gradually.

2 Press into the lined tin, prick with a fork and bake for 10–15 minutes until the shortbread is firm. Remove from the oven and leave to cool.

3 For the caramel layer, in a pan heat the brown sugar, butter, condensed milk and salt over a gentle heat until the butter has melted and the sugar dissolves. Bring to the boil, beating all the time so that the mixture doesn't burn then reduce the heat and simmer for about 5 minutes until the caramel is golden brown and thick. Pour over the shortbread and leave to cool in the refrigerator.

4 Place the white chocolate in a heatproof bowl over a pan of simmering water and stir until melted. Pour the chocolate over the caramel and leave to set in the refrigerator. Remove the lining paper and then cut into 24 squares. This will keep stored in the refrigerator for up to 3 days.

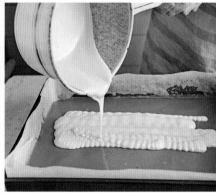

COCONUT mint slice

Coconut and mint are perhaps not a combination that you would often put together but they marry well in this rich and indulgent slice. It has pretty brown and white layers and will look elegant displayed on your cake stall.

PREPARATION TIME 30 minutes
BAKING TIME 15–20 minutes
MAKES about 20

EQUIPMENT 35 x 25cm/14 x 10in deep baking tin/pan, greased and lined
PREHEAT THE OVEN TO 180°C/350°F/Gas 4

FOR THE COCONUT BASE

225g/8oz/1 stick 7 tbsp butter, margarine or low-fat baking spread

170g/6oz/¾ cup caster/superfine sugar

225g/8oz/generous 1½ cups plain/all-purpose flour

60g/2oz/½ cup cocoa powder

100g/3½oz desiccated/dry unsweetened shredded coconut

FOR THE PEPPERMINT LAYER

350g/11½oz/3 cups icing/confectioners' sugar, sifted

50g/1¾oz/3 tbsp butter, softened

1 tsp/5ml peppermint extract

1 tbsp/15ml cream cheese

1–2 tbsp/15–30ml milk

FOR THE GANACHE

200g/7oz plain/semisweet chocolate (preferably 70% cocoa solids)

2 tbsp/30ml butter

2 tbsp/30ml milk

1 For the coconut base, cream together the butter or baking spread and caster sugar until light and creamy. Sift in the flour and cocoa powder and whisk in with the desiccated coconut until you have a soft dough.

2 Spoon the dough into the prepared tin and press out with your fingertips, dusting your hands with flour if the mixture is too sticky. You can press it out flat using a sheet of baking parchment on top if you wish.

3 Bake in the oven for 15–20 minutes until the coconut base is firm. Leave to cool completely.

4 For the peppermint layer, whisk together the sifted icing sugar, softened butter, peppermint extract, cream cheese and milk until very light and creamy. It is best to do this with an electric mixer. Spread the icing over the coconut base and chill in the refrigerator for about an hour.

5 For the ganache, break the chocolate into pieces and place in a heatproof bowl over a pan of simmering water with the butter and milk. Stir until the butter and chocolate have melted and you have a smooth glossy sauce. Leave until just cool and then spread over the icing. Return to the refrigerator and leave to set for at least 3 hours or overnight.

6 Remove the lining paper and cut into about 20 slices using a sharp knife and serve. This slice will store in an airtight container in the refrigerator for up to 3 days.

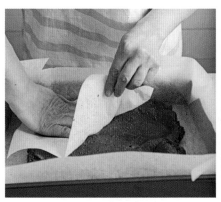

CORNFLAKE
raspberry layer tart

Cornflake traybake is a classic school dinner treat – with its irresistible layers of shortcake, jam and gooey cornflakes. When I brought it out for people to try there were cries of "I haven't had this since I was at school" – a long-lost treat of the past! The addition of lemon cuts through the sweetness of the syrup and reminds me of treacle tart. This is perfect to serve at a fête as it needs no decoration and once cooled is set firm so easily cuts into squares. It is also great served with custard, although that takes it into pudding rather than traybake territory!

PREPARATION TIME 20 minutes
BAKING TIME 20–30 minutes
MAKES 24

250g/8⅓oz/2 sticks butter, margarine or low-fat baking spread, softened

100g/3½oz/generous ¾ cups icing/confectioners' sugar, sifted

250g/9oz/1¾ cups plain/all-purpose flour, plus extra for dusting

A pinch of salt

100ml/4 heaped tbsp raspberry jam

FOR THE CORNFLAKE LAYER

200g/7oz golden/light corn syrup

85g/3oz/6 tbsp butter, margarine or low-fat baking spread

60g/2oz/¼ cup caster/superfine sugar

Zest of 1 lemon

200g/7oz/8 cups cornflakes

EQUIPMENT 35 x 25cm/14 x 10in deep baking tin/pan, greased and lined, cake cases
PREHEAT THE OVEN TO 180°C/350°F/Gas 4

1 Whisk together the butter and icing sugar until light and creamy. Sift the flour and whisk into the butter mixture with the salt. Press the soft dough into the lined tin in an even layer using a spatula – it will be very soft so dust your hands with a little flour so that it does not stick.

2 Bake in the oven for 15–20 minutes until lightly golden brown. Remove from the oven and leave to cool for a few minutes, leaving the oven on.

3 For the cornflake layer, heat the syrup, sugar and butter in a pan until the sugar and butter have melted. Stir in the lemon zest and cornflakes and mix well so that all the flakes are coated in the syrup.

4 Spread the jam out in an even layer over the shortcake base. Spoon over the cornflake mixture and spread out evenly, pressing down with the back of a spoon to compact it. Bake in the oven for a further 5–10 minutes, then leave to cool completely. The cornflake layer will set crisp as the traybake cools.

5 Remove the lining paper and cut into 24 squares to serve. This traybake will store for up to 3 days in an airtight container.

Hint and tip
You can use any jam you like for this recipe. For a chocolate version add a few tablespoons of cocoa powder to the syrup mixture before stirring in the cornflakes. This goes really well with cherry jam.

STRAWBERRY crumble squares

Hint and tip
You can replace the strawberries with raspberries or slices of fresh ripe peaches or nectarines if you wish.

This layered slice is inspired by my travels to Cyprus. In addition to lying by the pool and drinking iced coffee, one of the highlights was a strawberry tart that was served every morning at breakfast. It was utterly lovely and a very indulgent treat so early in the day. The base of this traybake is a buttery shortcake, topped with ripe berries and cheesecake cream and then finally sprinkled with a pine nut crumble layer. The smell of sweet strawberries when you take this from the oven will get your tastebuds tingling.

PREPARATION TIME 30 minutes
BAKING TIME 35–40 minutes
SERVES 24

300g/10oz/scant 2½ cups plain/all-purpose flour

1 tsp/5ml baking powder

170g/6oz/scant 1 cup dark brown sugar

180g/6oz/1½ sticks butter, margarine or low-fat baking spread, chilled

1 egg

60g/2oz/½ cup pine nuts

FOR THE STRAWBERRY LAYER

300g/10oz low-fat cream cheese

115g/4oz/½ cup caster/superfine sugar

2 eggs

500g/1¼lb ripe strawberries

2 tbsp/30ml cornflour/cornstarch

EQUIPMENT 35 x 25cm/14 x 10in deep baking tin/pan, greased and lined
PREHEAT THE OVEN TO 180°C/350°F/Gas 4

1 Sift the flour and baking powder into a bowl and stir in the sugar. Cut the butter into cubes and rub into the flour mixture with your fingertips until it resembles fine breadcrumbs. Beat the egg and mix into the crumbs which should come into larger clumps. Reserve a quarter of the crumbs for the topping and press the rest firmly into the base of the lined tin in an even layer with your fingertips.

2 For the strawberry layer, in a mixing bowl, whisk together the cream cheese, half of the caster sugar and the eggs until you have a smooth mixture.

3 Hull and halve the strawberries. Place in a bowl and sift over the cornflour and the remaining caster sugar and leave for a few minutes. Stir the fruit to ensure that it is all coated in the cornflour and the sugar.

4 Sprinkle the strawberries over the shortcake base and spoon over the cream cheese mixture. Mix lightly together. Sprinkle over the remaining crumb mixture and the pine nuts.

5 Bake for 35–40 minutes until the top is lightly golden brown then leave to cool completely before serving. Remove the lining paper and cut into 24 squares to serve. Store any uneaten cakes in the refrigerator for up to 3 days but this is best eaten on the day it is made.

CHERRY OREO
coconut slice

Cherries and chocolate are always a winning combination. This traybake has a buttery biscuit base and a coconut macaroon topping with a fruit middle layer of cherry jam and dried cherries. The whisked egg whites in the macaroon topping give a lightness to the slice so make sure that you whisk them well. If you don't have Oreos you can easily substitute digestive biscuits/graham crackers instead for the base, with a spoonful of cocoa powder if you wish.

PREPARATION TIME 20 minutes
BAKING TIME 15–20 minutes
MAKES 24

300g/10oz chocolate sandwich cookies, preferably Oreos

150g/5oz/1 stick 2 tbsp butter, margarine or low-fat baking spread

340g/12oz red cherry jam

150g/5oz dried cherries

75g/2½oz plain/semisweet chocolate, melted

FOR THE COCONUT LAYER

2 egg whites

200g/7oz/2⅔ cups soft shredded coconut (such as Angel Flake)

400g/14oz can of condensed milk

EQUIPMENT food processor, 35 x 25cm/14 x 10in deep baking tin/pan, greased and lined
PREHEAT THE OVEN TO 180°C/350°F/Gas 4

1 In a food processor, blitz the cookies to fine crumbs. If you do not have a food processor you can place the cookies in a clean plastic food bag and bash them with a rolling pin. Melt the butter in a pan and stir into the crumbs so that they are all coated. Tip the buttery crumbs into the lined tin and press out in an even layer using the back of a spoon.

2 Spread the cherry jam out in a layer over the biscuit base using a knife or spoon. Sprinkle over the dried cherries so that they are evenly distributed.

3 For the coconut layer, whisk the egg whites to stiff peaks in a clean dry bowl using an electric whisk. Mix the coconut and condensed milk together in a bowl. Add a large spoonful of the whisked egg whites and fold in to loosen the mixture. Add the remaining egg whites and fold in gently. Spoon the coconut mixture over the top of the jam and spread out evenly.

4 Bake in the oven for 15–20 minutes until the coconut layer is set and has turned lightly golden brown. Drizzle the top with thin lines of the melted chocolate using a fork and leave to cool in the refrigerator. When cool remove the lining paper and cut into 24 slices to serve. This slice will keep for up to 3 days in an airtight container.

Hint and tip
To make this recipe gluten-free use gluten-free sandwich cookies or gluten-free chocolate digestives. Also make sure the cherries do not have a wheat-based anti-caking agent.

LEMON
meringue slices

Lemon meringue pie is one of the most popular desserts and this traybake, inspired by that citrusy treat, is sure to sell well at any cake sale. It has a biscuit base made with digestives and a light lemon macaron layer topped with crushed meringue. Yum, yum!

LAYER TRAYBAKES

PREPARATION TIME 20 minutes
BAKING TIME 35–40 minutes
MAKES 24

EQUIPMENT food processor/blender, 35 x 25cm/14 x 10in deep baking tin/pan, greased and lined
PREHEAT THE OVEN TO 180°C/350°F/Gas 4

300g/10oz digestive biscuits/graham crackers

125g/4½oz/1 stick butter, margarine or low-fat baking spread

300g/10oz good quality lemon curd

FOR THE TOPPING

5 eggs

150g/5oz/¾ cup caster/superfine sugar

150g/5oz/1½ cups ground almonds

Zest of 2 lemons

3 meringue nests

1. Blitz the biscuits to fine crumbs in a blender or place in a clean plastic food bag and bash with a rolling pin. Heat the butter in a pan and then stir into the crumbs. Stir well so that all the crumbs are coated. Tip the crumbs into the base of the tin and press in firmly with the back of a spoon.

2. Spoon the lemon curd over the top of the biscuit base and spread out in an even layer.

3. For the topping, place the eggs and caster sugar in a stand mixer bowl and whisk for about 10 minutes until the mixture is very thick and creamy. You can do this using an electric hand whisk but I would not recommend doing this with a balloon whisk (or other non-electric whisk) as it will take a long time and your arm will hurt!

4. Fold the ground almonds and lemon zest into the egg mixture gently until incorporated. Pour the mixture into the tin and spread level with a spatula. Crush the meringues into small pieces and sprinkle over the top of the cake in the tin.

5. Bake in the oven for 15 minutes then turn the temperature down to 140°C/275°F/Gas 1 and bake for a further 20–25 minutes. Remove from the oven and leave to cool.

6. Once cool cut the cake into 24 slices and remove the lining paper. This cake will store for up to 3 days in an airtight container.

Hint and tip
If you want to reduce the calories in this slice, then use half of the lemon curd and spread it out thinly rather than in a thick layer.

SEVEN-LAYER
caramel nut bar

This American classic blows my mind every time I eat it. What possessed someone to layer up so many delicious things and bake them with condensed milk is beyond me – think cheesecake biscuit base piled high with coconut chocolate and then butterscotch or fudge pieces. This is one treat to save for special occasions when you want to indulge, but a book on traybakes would not be complete without it – in my view the Queen of Traybakes!

PREPARATION TIME 10 minutes
BAKING TIME 25–30 minutes
MAKES 24

300g/10½oz digestive biscuits/
graham crackers

150g/5oz/1 stick 2 tbsp butter,
margarine or low-fat baking spread

200g/7oz chocolate chips

100g/3½oz fudge pieces or
butterscotch chips

60g/2oz raisins

100g/3½oz/¾ cup pecans, coarsely
chopped

150g/5oz/2 cups soft shredded
coconut (such as Angel Flake)

60g/2oz toasted hazelnuts, halved or
roughly chopped

400g/14oz can of condensed milk

EQUIPMENT food processor or blender, 35 x 25cm/14 x 10in deep baking tin/pan, greased and lined
PREHEAT THE OVEN TO 180°C/350°F/Gas 4

1 Blitz the biscuits to fine crumbs in a food processor or blender. Alternatively place the biscuits in a clean plastic food bag and bash with a rolling pin. Melt the butter in a pan and pour into the crumbs. Stir well so that all the crumbs are coated in the butter. Press the crumbs out in an even layer over the base of the prepared tin using the back of a spoon.

2 Sprinkle the chocolate chips over the biscuit base in an even layer. Then spoon over the fudge pieces or butterscotch chips, raisins and pecans. Sprinkle over the coconut and hazelnuts.

3 Drizzle the whole cake with the condensed milk. Bake for 25–30 minutes until golden brown then leave to cool completely in the tin.

4 Cut into 24 squares to serve, removing the lining paper. This layer traybake will store in an airtight container for up to 3 days but I have never known it last that long!

SWEETIE patchwork cake

Three boys Robert, Ryan and Rousso sampled this cake for me as my taste testers and declared that it was "The best cake ever" – a definite thumbs up! This traybake is a real party piece, with a pretty patchwork decoration on top. You can use any sweets and candies you have in your cupboard for the decoration.

PREPARATION TIME 20 minutes
BAKING TIME 25–30 minutes
MAKES 24

340g/12oz/1½ cups caster/superfine sugar

340g/12oz/2 sticks 6 tbsp butter, margarine or low-fat baking spread, softened

6 eggs

340g/12oz/2½ cups self-raising/self-rising flour, sifted

150ml/¼ pint/⅔ cup natural/plain low-fat yogurt

Zest of 2 lemons and 1 orange

A few drops of orange food colouring gel

FOR THE FROSTING

500g/1¼lb/4 cups icing/confectioners' sugar, sifted

2 tbsp/30ml lemon curd

50g/1¾oz/3 tbsp butter, softened

1–2 tbsp/15–30ml milk

TO DECORATE

12 red liquorice laces

Colourful sweets/candies and sprinkles

EQUIPMENT 35 x 25cm/14 x 10in deep baking tin/pan, greased and lined
PREHEAT THE OVEN TO 180°C/350°F/Gas 4

1 To prepare the sponge, whisk together the caster sugar and the butter in a mixing bowl using a mixer or whisk until light and creamy. Add the eggs and whisk again. Fold in the sifted flour, yogurt, and lemon and orange zest. Divide the cake batter in two and colour one with a few drops of orange food colouring gel.

2 Spoon the orange cake batter into the prepared tin and spread out in an even layer using a spatula. Spoon the uncoloured batter on top, again spreading out in an even layer on top of the orange sponge.

3 Bake in the preheated oven for 25–30 minutes until the cake is firm and springs back to your touch. Remove from the oven and leave to cool for a few minutes, then turn out on to a rack to cool completely.

4 For the frosting, place the sifted icing sugar, lemon curd, butter and a little milk in a bowl and whisk to a smooth thick icing. If the frosting is too stiff add a little more milk and if it is too runny add a little more icing sugar. The consistency of the frosting will depend on how soft your butter is.

5 Place the cake on a serving plate or tray and spread the frosting over the top of the cake. Place 7 liquorice laces at even intervals along the long side of the cake and repeat on the short side with 5 laces, trimmed to fit. This will give you a lattice pattern of 24 squares, as shown in the photograph.

6 Working quickly whilst the frosting is still soft, decorate each square with different sweets and sprinkles to make a patchwork pattern. You can use dolly mixtures, sprinkles, chocolate buttons, sugar pips – anything you want really. Leave the cake to set. This cake will keep for up to 2 days in an airtight container but is best eaten on the day it is made.

Hints and tips

For a lower fat version 1) use low-fat baking spread in place of the butter 2) halve the icing quantity and just spread a thin layer of icing over the top of the cake.

VIRTUOUS
Traybakes

This is the chapter which allows you to have your cake and eat it! It contains healthier adaptations, lower in calories and lighter in sugar and fat. Just because you want a cake with lower calories should not mean you have to compromise on taste, and the recipes in this chapter give you some delicious alternatives that are sure to delight. There are also gluten-free, dairy-free and even egg-free traybakes for those on special diets. This chapter contains recipes for skinny lime and coconut drizzle cake, a low-fat dairy-free courgette cake, skinny blueberry traybake and a gluten-free grapefruit polenta cake.

There's no need to compromise on flavour with these delectable treats that are healthier for you too.

The flavours of cinnamon and chocolate always remind me of Christmas morning.

We ate it warm
at my village
sewing circle
and everyone
loved it!

I love a good
coffee cake and
this one is no
exception.

Skinny
LIME AND COCONUT
drizzle cake

This cake is adapted from a recipe given to me by the most amazing lady who lives in my village – Margaret Smith. She is an incredible cook, and she regularly makes this sponge for our village sewing circle as a sandwich cake layered with raspberries and cream (not quite so skinny but still gluten-free!). The traybake has a light texture and is topped with a little coconut for added texture. Finished with a tangy lime drizzle it tastes delicious and is virtually "sin" free.

PREPARATION TIME 15 minutes
BAKING TIME 30–35 minutes
MAKES 24

Sunflower oil for greasing

5 eggs

120g/4oz/generous ½ cup caster/superfine sugar

120g/4oz/1¼ cups ground almonds

Zest and juice of 2 limes

100g/3½oz/1⅓ cups soft shredded coconut (such as Angel Flake)

50g/1¾oz/⅓ cup icing/confectioners' sugar, sifted

EQUIPMENT 35 x 25cm/14 x 10in deep baking tin/pan
PREHEAT THE OVEN TO 180°C/350°F/Gas 4

1 Grease the tin with a little sunflower oil (do not use butter or margarine for greasing if you are baking this cake for someone who is allergic to dairy products). Line the baking tin.

2 Place the eggs and caster sugar in a stand mixer bowl and whisk for about 5 minutes until the mixture is very thick and creamy. You can do this using an electric hand whisk but I would not recommend doing this with a balloon whisk (or other non-electric whisk) as it will take a long time.

3 Fold the ground almonds and lime zest into the egg mixture gently until incorporated. Pour the mixture into the tin and spread level with a spatula. Sprinkle the coconut over the top of the cake.

4 Bake in the oven for 30–35 minutes until lightly golden brown on top and the cake springs back to your touch. If the coconut starts to brown too much before the cake is cooked, cover loosely with a sheet of foil.

5 In a pan heat the lime juice and icing sugar and bring to the boil. Drizzle over the cake and leave to cool. Cut the cake into 24 squares. Slide a sharp knife under each square of cake to release it from the paper. This gluten-free traybake can be a little fragile so place it on to a paper napkin or in a cake case to serve. It will store for up to 2 days in an airtight container but is best eaten on the day it is made.

dairy-free,
gluten-free

Skinny

BLUEBERRY
and cinnamon cake

This is a very skinny traybake with only 70 calories per slice – so good you can afford to have two! The fresh blueberries give bursts of natural sweetness to a light and airy sponge. Raspberries also work well, or you could replace the cinnamon with a little almond extract for a frangipane cake. It is gluten- and dairy-free.

VIRTUOUS TRAYBAKES

PREPARATION TIME 20 minutes
BAKING TIME 35–40 minutes
MAKES 24

Sunflower oil for greasing

5 eggs

120g/4oz/½ cup dark brown sugar

60g/2oz/generous ½ cup ground almonds

85g/3oz/¾ cup gluten-free self-raising/self-rising flour

1 tsp/5ml ground cinnamon

180g/6½oz/2 cups fresh blueberries

EQUIPMENT 35 x 25cm/14 x 10in deep baking tin/pan, cake cases
PREHEAT THE OVEN TO 180°C/350°F/Gas 4

1 Grease the tin with a little sunflower oil (do not use butter or margarine for greasing if you are baking this cake for someone who is allergic to dairy products). Line the baking tin.

2 Place the eggs and dark brown sugar in a stand mixer bowl and whisk for about 5 minutes until the mixture is very thick and creamy. You can do this using an electric hand whisk but I would not recommend doing this with a balloon whisk (or other non-electric whisk) as it will take a long time.

3 Fold the ground almonds, self-raising flour and ground cinnamon into the egg mixture gently until incorporated. Spoon the mixture into the tin and spread level with a spatula. Sprinkle the blueberries evenly over the cake.

4 Bake in the oven for 35–40 minutes until lightly golden brown on top and the cake springs back to your touch. Leave to cool completely. Cut the cake into 24 squares.

5 Slide a sharp knife under each square of cake to release it from the paper. As the cake contains no gluten the cake can be a little fragile so lift each slice carefully and place in a cake case to serve. This traybake will store for up to 2 days in an airtight container but is best eaten on the day it is made.

Only
70 calories
a slice!

Low-fat,
dairy-free,
gluten-free

COUGETTE SULTANA
and lemon cake

With the addition of courgette and sultanas a slice of this cake even contributes towards your 5-a-day. Do not be put off by the addition of the vegetable, you cannot taste it and it just makes the cake nice and moist. Take care that the icing sugar you use is gluten-free as some contain a wheat-based anti-caking agent.

PREPARATION TIME 20 minutes
BAKING TIME 35–40 minutes
MAKES 24

5 eggs

200g/7oz/1 cup caster/superfine sugar

200g/7oz/2 cups ground almonds

1 tsp/5ml baking powder

½ tsp/2.5ml bicarbonate of soda/baking soda

250g/9oz courgette/zucchini

150g/5oz sultanas/golden raisins

Finely grated zest of 2 lemons

Icing/confectioners' sugar, for dusting

EQUIPMENT 35 x 25cm/14 x 10in deep baking tin/pan, greased and lined, 24 muffin cases
PREHEAT THE OVEN TO 180°C/350°F/Gas 4

1 Whisk the eggs and caster sugar for 5 minutes until very light and creamy. It is important to whisk in as much air as possible as this will give lightness to the cake. Gently fold in the ground almonds, baking powder and bicarbonate of soda with a spatula.

2 Trim away the ends of the courgette and discard. Grate the courgettes and place in a square of muslin, cheesecloth or clean dish towel and squeeze out as much moisture as possible. Mix the grated courgette with the sultanas and lemon zest and gently fold into the cake mixture. Pour the mixture into the tin and bake for 35–40 minutes. Leave to cool, it will sink but this is normal.

3 Dust the cake with icing sugar and cut into 24 squares. The cake is slightly fragile, so place each piece in a muffin case. This traybake will store for up to 2 days in an airtight container but is best eaten on the day it is made.

Hint and tip

To reduce calories further omit the glaze and just dust the cake with a very thin layer of icing sugar instead. If the glaze seems too thin add a little more icing sugar.

Gluten-free CHOCOLATE and cinnamon cake

The flavours of cinnamon and chocolate always remind me of Christmas morning, eating chocolate coins from our stockings and the house filled with the delicious cinnamon scents of Christmas baking. This traybake is light and moist from the ground almonds and you would never know it is gluten-free.

PREPARATION TIME 20 minutes
BAKING TIME 25–35 minutes
MAKES 24

225g/8oz/1 stick 7 tbsp low-fat baking spread, softened

225g/8oz/1 cup caster/superfine sugar

4 eggs

175g/6oz/1¼ cups gluten-free self-raising/self-rising flour

60g/2oz/½ cup gluten-free cocoa powder

2 tsp/10ml ground cinnamon

150g/5oz/1½ cups ground almonds

250ml/8fl oz/1 cup zero-fat or low-fat natural/plain yogurt

Sugared chocolate sweets/candies, to decorate (optional)

FOR THE GLAZE

85g/3oz/⅔ cups cocoa powder

60g/2oz icing/confectioners' sugar

85g/3oz/⅔ stick butter or low-fat baking spread, softened

Juice of 3 large oranges

4 tbsp/60ml agave nectar

EQUIPMENT 35 x 25cm/14 x 10in deep baking tin/pan, greased and lined, cooling rack, fine mesh sieve/strainer, foil
PREHEAT THE OVEN TO 180°C/350°F/Gas 4

1 In a mixing bowl, whisk together the low-fat baking spread and sugar until very light and creamy. Add the eggs, one at a time, whisking after each one is added.

2 Sift in the flour, cocoa and cinnamon and add the ground almonds and yogurt. Fold in gently. Spoon into the prepared tin in an even layer with a spatula and bake in the oven for 25–35 minutes until the cake is firm and springs back to your touch. Turn the cake out on to a rack and leave to cool.

3 For the glaze, sift together the cocoa powder and icing sugar and place with all the remaining ingredients in a pan and heat until the butter has melted and the sauce is thin and glossy. Pass the mixture through a fine mesh sieve to remove any lumps.

4 Once the cake is cool, place a sheet of foil underneath the rack to catch any glaze so that you do not make a mess. Pour the glaze over the top of the cake, it will soak in. Place the traybake on a chopping board, cut into 24 squares and place sweets on top of each cake to decorate, if you wish.

GRAPEFRUIT
and poppy seed polenta cake

It is not very often that you come across grapefruit cake and as I was testing recipes for the book, I discovered that there may well be a good reason for this as grapefruit can be notoriously bitter. I did however persevere as grapefruit was my Grandma's favourite and I wanted to include something she would have loved. Eventually this traybake was born. We ate it warm at my village sewing circle and everyone loved it! My friend John Marshall suggested grapefruit drizzle cake so I owe him full credit for the inspiration.

Hint and tip
You can make a lemon version of this cake using lemon zest in the cake and the juice of 3 lemons for the drizzle. Oranges also work well.

PREPARATION TIME 30 minutes
BAKING TIME 30–40 minutes
MAKES 24

225g/8oz/1 stick 7 tbsp low-fat baking spread, softened

170g/6oz/generous ¾ cup caster/superfine sugar, plus 100g/3½oz/½ cup for sugar syrup

60g/2oz/¼ cup dark brown sugar

Zest of 1 red grapefruit, plus extra to decorate

3 eggs

200g/7oz/2 cups ground almonds

150g/5oz polenta grains

1 tsp/5ml baking powder

125ml/4fl oz/½ cup low-fat natural/plain yogurt

28g/1oz/2 tbsp poppy seeds

24 red grapefruit segments

Juice of 2 red grapefruits

2 tbsp/30ml icing/confectioners' sugar

EQUIPMENT 35 x 25cm/14 x 10in deep baking tin/pan, greased and lined
PREHEAT THE OVEN TO 180°C/350°F/Gas 4

1 Whisk together the baking spread, caster sugar and dark brown sugar until light and creamy. Add the grapefruit zest and eggs and whisk again well until the eggs are all incorporated. Add the ground almonds, polenta grains and baking powder with the yogurt and whisk in. Fold through the poppy seeds and pour the mixture into the baking tin.

2 Bake for 30–40 minutes until the top of the cake is golden brown and the cake springs back to your touch. Remove from the oven.

3 Prepare a citrus drizzle straight away by heating the grapefruit juice with the icing sugar and bringing just to the boil. Spoon the hot drizzle over the warm cake making sure that the whole top is covered. Do not oversoak the cake though. You may not need all of the drizzle depending on how much juice your grapefruits contain. Leave to cool.

4 To make the candied zest for decoration, simmer 250ml/8fl oz/1 cup water with the remaining caster sugar until the sugar has dissolved. Peel thin strands of zest with a julienne peeler, making sure that you have the zest only and not the pith. Simmer for about 2–3 minutes in the hot syrup until the zest is soft.

5 When cool cut the traybake into 24 squares and decorate with grapefruit segments and zest. It will store for up to 3 days in an airtight container.

PEACH MELBA cake

Dame Nellie Melba was an amazing singer and it is said that one day she had a sore throat and to treat it a chef created a delicious peach dessert with vanilla ice cream to soothe her throat – and so the classic Peach Melba was born. Inspired by that dessert, this traybake combines peaches and raspberries to give it the ultimate sunshine taste. If you are eating this cake at home why not serve with low-fat frozen yogurt in a true homage to the traditional peach melba.

VIRTUOUS TRAYBAKES

PREPARATION TIME 20 minutes
BAKING TIME 40–50 minutes
MAKES 24

225g/8oz/1 stick 7 tbsp low-fat baking spread, softened

225g/8oz/1 cup caster/superfine sugar

1 tsp/5ml almond extract

4 eggs

150g/5oz/1½ cups gluten-free self-raising/self-rising flour

150g/5oz/1½ cups ground almonds

1 tsp/5ml baking powder

250ml/8fl oz/1 cup zero-fat natural/plain yogurt

300g/10oz fresh raspberries

2–3 ripe peaches

Flaked/sliced almonds, to sprinkle

EQUIPMENT 35 x 25cm/14 x 10in deep baking tin/pan, greased and lined
PREHEAT THE OVEN TO 180°C/350°F/Gas 4

1 In a large mixing bowl, whisk together the low-fat baking spread and caster sugar until very pale and creamy. Whisk in the almond extract. Add the eggs one at a time, beating the mixture after each addition.

2 Sift in the gluten-free self-raising flour and fold in with the ground almonds and baking powder. Gently whisk in the yogurt. Spoon the mixture into the prepared tin and spread out level using a spatula.

3 Sprinkle the raspberries over the top of the cake. Cut the peaches into thin slices and place on top of the cake in between the raspberries in a pretty pattern. Sprinkle over the flaked almonds.

4 Bake in the oven for 40–50 minutes until the cake is golden brown on top and a knife comes out clean when inserted into the centre of the cake and it springs back to your touch.

5 Leave to cool in the tin and then remove the lining paper and cut into 24 slices to serve. This traybake will store for up to 3 days in an airtight container but is best eaten on the day it is made.

EGG-FREE
mini Victoria sponges

I am often asked if I can make egg-free cakes and I used to really worry about doing so as to me eggs are such an important ingredient for making a cake light and airy. However I need not have worried as this version tastes as good as a regular sponge cake, with air and lightness added by the bicarbonate of soda and baking powder. I served this traybake to friends and everyone said it was a wonderful Victoria sponge. I never let on it was egg-free!

PREPARATION TIME 20 minutes
BAKING TIME 40–50 minutes
MAKES 24

225g/8oz/1 stick 7 tbsp low-fat baking spread

225g/8oz/1 cup caster/superfine sugar

300g/10oz/2 cups self-raising/self-rising flour

½ tsp/2.5ml bicarbonate of soda/baking soda

1 tsp/5ml baking powder

1 tsp/5ml vanilla extract

125ml/4fl oz/½ cup skimmed milk

250ml/8fl oz/1 cup zero-fat natural/plain yogurt

4 tbsp/60ml raspberry, strawberry or cherry jam

Icing/confectioners' sugar, for dusting

EQUIPMENT 35 x 25cm/14 x 10in deep baking tin/pan, greased and lined
PREHEAT THE OVEN TO 180°C/350°F/Gas 4

1 Whisk the low-fat baking spread and sugar for about 5 minutes until very light and creamy. It is important to whisk in as much air as possible as this will give lightness to the cake. Sift together the self-raising flour, bicarbonate of soda and baking powder and then whisk into the creamed butter mixture.

2 Add the vanilla, milk and yogurt and whisk in. Spoon the mixture into the prepared tin and bake for 40–50 minutes until the cake is firm and springs back to your touch and a knife comes out clean when inserted into the middle of the cake. Leave to cool.

3 Cut the cake in half so that you have two rectangles and spread the jam over one of the halves. Place the second rectangle on top and cut into 24 squares. Dust with a little icing sugar to serve. This cake will keep for up to 2 days in an airtight container.

Hint and tip

If you want to vary the flavour of this cake, you can add chocolate chips, citrus zest or substitute 30g/¼oz of the self-raising/self-rising flour with sifted cocoa powder.

EGG-FREE
coffee cake

I love a good coffee cake and this one is no exception. It is light and airy despite the lack of eggs, and has a yummy coffee flavour from espresso and coffee granules. If you do not have an espresso machine at home, simply add an extra teaspoon of coffee granules or a teaspoon of coffee extract instead. The cake can be baked with a sprinkling of chocolate chips on top for an extra mocha treat, although this will increase the calorie content. For a skinny version omit the cream cheese frosting.

VIRTUOUS TRAYBAKES

PREPARATION TIME 20 minutes
BAKING TIME 40–50 minutes
MAKES 24

1 tsp/5ml instant coffee granules

60ml/2fl oz/¼ cup hot espresso coffee

225g/8oz/1 stick 7 tbsp low-fat baking spread, softened

225g/8oz/1 cup caster/superfine sugar

300g/10oz/2 cups self-raising/self-rising flour

½ tsp/2.5ml bicarbonate of soda/baking soda

1 tsp/5ml baking powder

150g/5oz/1½ cups ground almonds

4 tbsp/60ml skimmed milk

250ml/8fl oz/1 cup zero-fat or low-fat natural/plain yogurt

Chocolate coffee beans, to decorate

FOR THE FROSTING

300g/10oz/2 cups icing/confectioners' sugar, sifted

60g/2oz cream cheese

30g/1oz butter

Juice of 1 lemon

EQUIPMENT 35 x 25cm/14 x 10in deep baking tin/pan, greased and lined, piping/pastry bag, star nozzle
PREHEAT THE OVEN TO 180°C/350°F/Gas 4

1 Dissolve the coffee granules in the hot espresso and leave to cool. If you do not have espresso simply dissolve 2 tsp/10ml coffee granules in 60ml/2fl oz/¼ cup of boiling water.

2 Whisk the low-fat baking spread and sugar for 5 minutes until very light and creamy. It is important to whisk in as much air as possible as this will give lightness to the cake. Sift together the self-raising flour, bicarbonate of soda and baking powder and then whisk into the creamed baking spread mixture with the almonds and the coffee.

3 Add the milk and yogurt and whisk in. Spoon the mixture into the prepared tin and spread out. Bake for 40–50 minutes until the cake is firm and springs back to your touch and a knife comes out clean with no batter on when inserted into the centre of the cake. Leave to cool.

4 For the cream cheese frosting, place the sifted icing sugar, cream cheese, butter and lemon juice into a mixing bowl and whisk together until thick and creamy. If the frosting is too stiff add a little more lemon juice and if it is too runny add a little more sifted icing sugar.

5 Remove the lining paper and then cut the cake into 24 slices. Pipe a little cream cheese frosting on each slice using the piping bag and star nozzle and top with chocolate coffee beans for decoration. This cake will keep for up to 2 days in an airtight container.

NUTRITION NOTES

RED VELVET WITH CREAM CHEESE FROSTING (makes 24) Energy 374kcal/1571kJ; Protein 4.6g; Carbohydrate 52.5g, of which sugars 41.4g; Fat 17.7g, of which saturates 10.5g; Cholesterol 98mg; Calcium 80mg; Fibre 1g; Sodium 221mg.

BANANA SHEET CAKE (makes 24) Energy 274kcal/1147kJ; Protein 4.1g; Carbohydrate 35.5g, of which sugars 23.8g; Fat 13.7g, of which saturates 7.9g; Cholesterol 88mg; Calcium 83mg; Fibre 1.1g; Sodium 165mg.

GLAZED CINNAMON APPLE SLICE (makes 24) Energy 327kcal/1366kJ; Protein 6.3g; Carbohydrate 32.7g, of which sugars 21.6g; Fat 19.9g, of which saturates 9.4g; Cholesterol 93mg; Calcium 99mg; Fibre 1.2g; Sodium 199mg.

PUMPKIN GINGERBREAD (makes 24) Energy 246kcal/1035kJ; Protein 3.9g; Carbohydrate 35.9g, of which sugars 18.4g; Fat 10.7g, of which saturates 6.4g; Cholesterol 44mg; Calcium 105mg; Fibre 1.2g; Sodium 240mg.

ORANGE AND CHOCOLATE LAYER CAKE (makes 24) Energy 216kcal/900kJ; Protein 2.6g; Carbohydrate 19.1g, of which sugars 18.8g; Fat 14.9g, of which saturates 8.8g; Cholesterol 88mg; Calcium 19mg; Fibre 0.4g; Sodium 126mg.

RED, WHITE AND BLUE WAVE-THE-FLAG CAKE (makes 24) Energy 285kcal/1196kJ; Protein 2.6g; Carbohydrate 37g, of which sugars 36.8g; Fat 15.1g, of which saturates 9g; Cholesterol 93mg; Calcium 22mg; Fibre 0g; Sodium 136mg.

BLACKBERRY AND PASSION FRUIT SPONGE (makes 24) Energy 260kcal/1086kJ; Protein 3.5g; Carbohydrate 27.9g, of which sugars 16.5g; Fat 15.7g, of which saturates 9.4g; Cholesterol 74mg; Calcium 91mg; Fibre 1.6g; Sodium 174mg.

LAMINGTONS (makes 20) Energy 489kcal/2041kJ; Protein 5g; Carbohydrate 48.5g, of which sugars 35.8g; Fat 31.9g, of which saturates 21.7g; Cholesterol 110mg; Calcium 84mg; Fibre 3.9g; Sodium 214mg.

NELSON SLICE (makes 24) Energy 240kcal/1006kJ; Protein 3.5g; Carbohydrate 32.3g, of which sugars 15.9g; Fat 11g, of which saturates 4.8g; Cholesterol 33mg; Calcium 51mg; Fibre 1.2g; Sodium 200mg.

CHOCOLATE CHIP FLAPJACK (makes 24) Energy 264kcal/1106kJ; Protein 3.6g; Carbohydrate 34.7g, of which sugars 19.1g; Fat 13.3g, of which saturates 7.1g; Cholesterol 23mg; Calcium 23mg; Fibre 2.6g; Sodium 105mg.

CHERRY COMPOTE FLAPJACKS (makes 24) Energy 243kcal/1021kJ; Protein 2.9g; Carbohydrate 36.6g, of which sugars 21.4g; Fat 10.4g, of which saturates 5.4g; Cholesterol 22mg; Calcium 22mg; Fibre 2.3g; Sodium 83mg.

DOUBLE-GINGER FLAPJACK (makes 24) Energy 213kcal/895kJ; Protein 2.7g; Carbohydrate 29.1g, of which sugars 13.9g; Fat 10.4g, of which saturates 5.4g; Cholesterol 22mg; Calcium 17mg; Fibre 1.9g; Sodium 81mg.

LEMON AND SULTANA FLAPJACK (makes 24) Energy 236kcal/993kJ; Protein 2.9g; Carbohydrate 34.9g, of which sugars 19.7g; Fat 10.4g, of which saturates 5.4g; Cholesterol 22mg; Calcium 22mg; Fibre 2.1g; Sodium 82mg.

GRANOLA SQUARES (makes 24) Energy 202kcal/851kJ; Protein 2.9g; Carbohydrate 32g, of which sugars 16.1g; Fat 7.8g, of which saturates 4.4g; Cholesterol 18mg; Calcium 36mg; Fibre 1g; Sodium 78mg.

OATY APRICOT SLICE (makes 30) Energy 175kcal/734kJ; Protein 2.5g; Carbohydrate 22.5g, of which sugars 8.4g; Fat 9g, of which saturates 5.1g; Cholesterol 28mg; Calcium 27mg; Fibre 1.5g; Sodium 68mg.

APPLE SHORTCAKE (makes 24) Energy 225kcal/942kJ; Protein 1.8g; Carbohydrate 28.7g, of which sugars 16.4g; Fat 12.2g, of which saturates 7.6g; Cholesterol 31mg; Calcium 43mg; Fibre 1.6g; Sodium 111mg.

CRISPY TIFFIN SLICE (makes 24) Energy 296kcal/1243kJ; Protein 2.6g; Carbohydrate 39.8g, of which sugars 27.8g; Fat 15.2g, of which saturates 9.2g; Cholesterol 27mg; Calcium 61mg; Fibre 0.7g; Sodium 140mg.

CHOCOLATE AND CHERRY BROWNIES (makes 24) Energy 288kcal/1206kJ; Protein 3.6g; Carbohydrate 39.4g, of which sugars 33g; Fat 13.9g, of which saturates 8g; Cholesterol 81mg; Calcium 36mg; Fibre 1.2g; Sodium 88mg.

S'MORES BROWNIES (makes 24) Energy 297kcal/1244kJ; Protein 3.2g; Carbohydrate 36.6g, of which sugars 24g; Fat 16.3g, of which saturates 9.5g; Cholesterol 61mg; Calcium 32mg; Fibre 0.5g; Sodium 230mg.

PEPPERMINT BROWNIES (makes 24) Energy 277kcal/1155kJ; Protein 3.9g; Carbohydrate 28.3g, of which sugars 21.8g; Fat 17.3g, of which saturates 10.2g; Cholesterol 71mg; Calcium 52mg; Fibre 0.9g; Sodium 93mg.

SKINNY BANOFFEE BROWNIES (makes 24) Energy 141kcal/594kJ; Protein 3.7g; Carbohydrate 17.9g, of which sugars 11.6g; Fat 6.6g, of which saturates 1.8g; Cholesterol 49mg; Calcium 29mg; Fibre 0.9g; Sodium 121mg.

PECAN PIE BLONDIES (makes 24) Energy 332kcal/1383kJ; Protein 4.4g; Carbohydrate 30.6g, of which sugars 24.1g; Fat 22.1g, of which saturates 10.1g; Cholesterol 75mg; Calcium 70mg; Fibre 0.9g; Sodium 115mg.

PISTACHIO AND WHITE CHOCOLATE BLONDIE (makes 24) Energy 312kcal/1303kJ; Protein 4.4g; Carbohydrate 33.5g, of which sugars 25.4g; Fat 18.7g, of which saturates 8.4g; Cholesterol 61mg; Calcium 63mg; Fibre 1g; Sodium 126mg.

RASPBERRY CHEESECAKE BLONDIES (makes 24) Energy 240kcal/1000kJ; Protein 5.6g; Carbohydrate 22.2g, of which sugars 13.4g; Fat 14.9g, of which saturates 8.6g; Cholesterol 81mg; Calcium 74mg; Fibre 1g; Sodium 155mg.

COCONUT BLONDIE BROWNIES (makes 24) Energy 262kcal/1088kJ; Protein 4g; Carbohydrate 17.2g, of which sugars 10.8g; Fat 20.1g, of which saturates 13.2g; Cholesterol 71mg; Calcium 48mg; Fibre 2.1g; Sodium 93mg.

UPSIDE-DOWN MILLIONAIRE'S SHORTBREAD (makes 30) Energy 246kcal/1030kJ; Protein 3.9g; Carbohydrate 28.5g, of which sugars 20.6g; Fat 13.7g, of which saturates 8.5g; Cholesterol 29mg; Calcium 102mg; Fibre 0.9g; Sodium 127mg.

COCONUT MINT SLICE (makes 20) Energy 349kcal/1461kJ; Protein 2.6g; Carbohydrate 43.2g, of which sugars 34g; Fat 19.6g, of which saturates 13g; Cholesterol 34mg; Calcium 33mg; Fibre 2.2g; Sodium 129mg.

CORNFLAKE RASPBERRY LAYER TART (makes 24) Energy 233kcal/976kJ; Protein 1.8g; Carbohydrate 32.1g, of which sugars 17.3g; Fat 11.7g, of which saturates 7.3g; Cholesterol 30mg; Calcium 20mg; Fibre 0.7g; Sodium 193mg.

STRAWBERRY CRUMBLE SQUARES (makes 24) Energy 202kcal/846kJ; Protein 4.6g; Carbohydrate 25.1g, of which sugars 14.4g; Fat 9.9g, of which saturates 4.9g; Cholesterol 48mg; Calcium 45mg; Fibre 0.9g; Sodium 114mg.

CHERRY OREO COCONUT SLICE (makes 24) Energy 284kcal/1189kJ; Protein 3.3g; Carbohydrate 35g, of which sugars 30.3g; Fat 15.5g, of which saturates 10.7g; Cholesterol 26mg; Calcium 68mg; Fibre 1.8g; Sodium 95mg.

LEMON MERINGUE SLICES (makes 24) Energy 184kcal/771kJ; Protein 2.6g; Carbohydrate 25g, of which sugars 15.3g; Fat 8.8g, of which saturates 4.4g; Cholesterol 67mg; Calcium 23mg; Fibre 0g; Sodium 135mg.

SEVEN-LAYER CARAMEL NUT BAR (makes 24) Energy 310kcal/1295kJ; Protein 3.9g; Carbohydrate 29g, of which sugars 22g; Fat 20.7g, of which saturates 10.9g; Cholesterol 27mg; Calcium 77mg; Fibre 2g; Sodium 146mg.

SWEETIE PATCHWORK CAKE (makes 24) Energy 336kcal/1411kJ; Protein 3.7g; Carbohydrate 48.8g, of which sugars 37.7g; Fat 15.4g, of which saturates 9g; Cholesterol 93mg; Calcium 77mg; Fibre 0.6g; Sodium 179mg.

SKINNY LIME AND COCONUT DRIZZLE CAKE (makes 24) Energy 103kcal/428kJ; Protein 2.9g; Carbohydrate 8g, of which sugars 7.9g; Fat 6.8g, of which saturates 2.8g; Cholesterol 48mg; Calcium 22mg; Fibre 0.8g; Sodium 20mg.

SKINNY BLUEBERRY AND CINNAMON CAKE (makes 24) Energy 70kcal/294kJ; Protein 2.4g; Carbohydrate 9.2g, of which sugars 6.2g; Fat 2.9g, of which saturates 0.5g; Cholesterol 48mg; Calcium 27mg; Fibre 0.4g; Sodium 31mg.

COURGETTE SULTANA AND LEMON CAKE (makes 24) Energy 122kcal/511kJ; Protein 3.7g; Carbohydrate 13.8g, of which sugars 13.6g; Fat 6.1g, of which saturates 0.8g; Cholesterol 48mg; Calcium 36mg; Fibre 0.3g; Sodium 20mg.

GLUTEN-FREE CHOCOLATE AND CINNAMON CAKE (makes 24) Energy 249kcal/1039kJ; Protein 5g; Carbohydrate 21g, of which sugars 14.7g; Fat 16.7g, of which saturates 8.2g; Cholesterol 66mg; Calcium 76mg; Fibre 1.3g; Sodium 184mg.

GRAPEFRUIT AND POPPY SEED POLENTA CAKE (makes 24) Energy 109kcal/455kJ; Protein 2.9g; Carbohydrate 13.4g, of which sugars 8.9g; Fat 5.6g, of which saturates 1.2g; Cholesterol 30mg; Calcium 42mg; Fibre 0.4g; Sodium 76mg.

PEACH MELBA CAKE (makes 24) Energy 194kcal/811kJ; Protein 4g; Carbohydrate 17.4g, of which sugars 12.6g; Fat 12.5g, of which saturates 5.6g; Cholesterol 59mg; Calcium 68mg; Fibre 1g; Sodium 102mg.

EGG-FREE MINI VICTORIA SPONGES (makes 24) Energy 126kcal/534kJ; Protein 2.5g; Carbohydrate 22.2g, of which sugars 12.8g; Fat 3.7g, of which saturates 0.8g; Cholesterol 1mg; Calcium 72mg; Fibre 0.5g; Sodium 117mg.

EGG-FREE COFFEE CAKE (makes 24) Energy 146kcal/614kJ; Protein 3.4g; Carbohydrate 18.3g, of which sugars 11.1g; Fat 7.1g, of which saturates 1.1g; Cholesterol 1mg; Calcium 70mg; Fibre 0.4g; Sodium 105mg.

INDEX

Try Me!

This edition is published by Lorenz Books, an imprint of Anness Publishing Ltd
info@anness.com

www.lorenzbooks.com; www.annesspublishing.com

If you like the images in this book and would like to investigate using them for publishing, promotions or advertising, please visit our website www.practicalpictures.com for more information.

A CIP catalogue record for this book is available from the British Library.

Publisher: Joanna Lorenz
Photography and styling: Nicki Dowey
Food styling: Valerie Berry
Design: Jane McKenna (Fogdog.co.uk)
Editorial: Sarah Lumby

COOK'S NOTES
Bracketed terms are intended for American readers.

For all recipes, quantities are given in both metric and imperial measures and, where appropriate, in standard cups and spoons. Follow one set of measures, but not a mixture, because they are not interchangeable.

Standard spoon and cup measures are level. 1 tsp = 5ml, 1 tbsp = 15ml, 1 cup = 250ml/8fl oz.

Australian standard tablespoons are 20ml. Australian readers should use 3 tsp in place of 1 tbsp for measuring small quantities.

American pints are 16fl oz/2 cups. American readers should use 20fl oz/2.5 cups in place of 1 pint when measuring liquids.

Electric oven temperatures in this book are for conventional ovens. When using a fan oven, the temperature will probably need to be reduced by about 10–20°C/20–40°F. Since ovens vary, you should check with your manufacturer's instruction book for guidance.

The nutritional analysis given for each recipe is calculated per portion (i.e. serving or item), unless otherwise stated. If the recipe gives a range, such as Serves 4–6, then the nutritional analysis will be for the smaller portion size, i.e. 6 servings. The analysis does not include optional ingredients, such as additional decorations.

Medium (US large) eggs are used unless otherwise stated.